Introducing Child Care Social Work

Contemporary Policy and Practice

Post-qualifying Social Work Practice – titles in the series

To order, please contact our distributor: BEBC Distribution, Albion Close, Parkstone, Poole, BH12 3LL. Telephone: 0845 230 9000, email: **learningmatters@bebc.co.uk**.

You can also order online at **www.learningmatters.co.uk**.

Introducing
Child Care
Social Work
Contemporary Policy and Practice

JILL DAVEY AND JENNIFER BIGMORE

Series Editor: Keith Brown

LearningMatters

First published in 2009 by Learning Matters Ltd

British Library Cataloguing in Publication Data
A CIP record for this book is available from the British Library

ISBN 978 1 84445 180 7

Cover design by Code 5 Design Associates Ltd
Project management by Deer Park Productions, Tavistock
Typeset by PDQ Typesetting Ltd, Newcastle-under-Lyme
Printed and bound in Great Britain by Bell & Bain Ltd, Glasgow

Learning Matters Ltd
33 Southernhay East
Exeter EX1 1NX
Tel: 01392 215560
info@learningmatters.co.uk
www.learningmatters.co.uk

Mixed Sources
Product group from well-managed
forests and other controlled sources
www.fsc.org Cert no. TT-COC-002769
© 1996 Forest Stewardship Council

FSC

Contents

Foreword to the Post-Qualifying Social Work Practice series

All the texts in the Post-Qualifying Social Work Practice series have been written by people with a passion for excellence in social work practice. They are primarily written for social workers who are undertaking post-qualifying social work awards, but will also be useful to any social worker who wants to consider up-to-date practice issues.

The books in this series are also of value to social work students as they are written to inform, inspire and develop social work practice.

Keith Brown
Series Editor
Centre for Post-Qualifying Social Work, Bournemouth

About the authors

Jill Davey has been a qualified social worker for over 25 years and holds a master's degree in practice teaching. During her career she has held both strategic and managerial positions in relation to child protection, including a regional advisor's role with the DfES. Jill has worked in both education and social services within the specialism of Child Care. Jill was invited to join Bournemouth University as a senior lecturer six years ago to take a lead in writing and developing the Post-Qualifying Child Care Award.

Jennifer Bigmore is the course leader for the Post-Qualifying BA (Hons)/Graduate Diploma in Children and Family Studies at Bournemouth University. Having completed a master's degree in social work studies at Southampton University, she worked as a social worker in both education and child protection before joining Bournemouth University to develop and deliver the Post-Qualifying Child Care Award.

About the contributors

Vanessa Bomphrey is a social worker with many years of experience. She currently works for the Education Welfare Service and completed her Post-Qualifying Social Work Award in 2008.

Janet Cheeseright graduated from the University of Plymouth in 2002 with a BSc in Social Work and Social Policy with DipSW. She has been employed as a social worker within the Plymouth Youth Offending Service for the past seven years. Her role includes carrying out assessments of young people's criminogenic and other needs, and case-managing remand and bail support cases, community sentences and pre- and post-release supervision. She also prepares pre-sentence reports for Crown and Youth Courts. She has a varied caseload, working with both high and medium risk offenders.

Andrew Chipangura qualified as a social worker in 1988 in Zimbabwe and has worked in both the government and private sectors. He started work in the UK as a child care social worker. Andrew completed his Post-Qualifying Social Work Award in 2006. He is currently working in a field child care social work team and is studying for a diploma in employment law.

Mike Coleman qualified as a social worker in 2003 and completed his Post-Qualifying Social Work Award in 2006. Mike has worked for the local authority, primarily in child protection and court work, and he has recently begun working as a family court advisor for CAFCASS.

Denise Jackson is a practice manager employed by Cornwall's Children, Young People and Families Directorate and has worked with the Risk Assessment and Support Team since its inception in 2002. Denise is a registered social worker with 20 years' experience. Previous employment has been within the voluntary sector (Barnardo's) and as an independent therapist and trainer with the Lucy Faithfull Foundation, a leading UK charity working in the field of sexual aggression. Denise is also an expert witness to the courts.

Mary Jones began her social work career in the 1970s, completing a BSc in Psychology and Sociology at Brunel University in 1972. She completed an MA in Criminology at Sheffield University in 1975 and the CQSW at Sheffield University in 1978. Mary completed her Post-Qualifying Child Care Award in 2005. Her professional experience includes residential work in a girls' remand centre, a Rudolph Steiner School and a hostel for children with learning disabilities, as well as generic fieldwork in the West Riding of Yorkshire and ten years in Sheffield. She is currently senior social worker in a children in care team in Cornwall, where she has worked with children and families since 1988.

Yvonne Mieville is an experienced social worker working for Dorset County Council. She completed her Post-Qualifying Child Care Award in 2008 and is currently pursuing her studies at master's level. She plans to undertake a PhD in the future.

Steven Mills is an experienced social worker, currently working for Bournemouth Borough Council. Steven completed his Post-Qualifying Child Care Award in 2009.

Liz Reilly qualified as a social worker in 1999 after completing a graduate course in social work at the University of Bristol. She also completed a master's in Social Work at the same university, graduating in 2000. Before, during and after qualifying she worked with young people 'in and leaving care', and in various levels of supported and semi-independent living. In particular, she worked as a social worker and a deputy manager for North Somerset Council's Leaving Care Service. Since October 2008, Liz has been studying for the Post-Qualifying Specialist Child Care Award and, at the same time, is working as a social worker in an assessment team. Other interests include community-based social work, Family Group Conference models of engaging families and, more recently, about the development of social work as a technical activity.

Hilary Schultess-Young qualified 13 years ago and has practised in Cornwall County Council's Social Care Department since that time. She has held a number of posts in children's services including Youth Offending, Access and Assessment and, as a specialist worker, with Gypsies and Travellers. Hilary is currently a specialist Hidden Harm social worker, piloting a project for the local authority which provides intensive intervention work with families and addresses parental substance use issues and their impact upon children and young people subject to a child protection plan or in care.

Trevor Thomas qualified as a social worker in 1988 and started his practice as a deputy social worker for Worcester County Council where he gained invaluable experience in child protection. In 2003, Trevor relocated to the then North Cornwall children's team, working across access and assessment as well as working with long-term cases. Upon completion of the Post-Qualifying Child Care Award, Trevor became practice manager within his team with responsibilities for access and assessment. Trevor now works as an independent reviewing manager for Cornwall County Council, reviewing the cases of children in care and chairing child protection conferences.

Andrea Wilkinson has been a qualified social worker for the last seven years. She started her social work career working in adult social care which, prior to 2005, met the needs of both adults and children with learning disabilities in Cornwall. She worked predominantly with disabled children, children with complex needs and children with life-limiting illnesses at this time. In 2005, Disabled Children in Cornwall became part of children's services and children no longer had their needs met within adult teams. Instead, Community Support Teams were formed to meet the needs of children with disabilities. Andrea is due to take up a new role within Children, Schools and Families Services in Cornwall in the post of Senior Social Worker Disability Lead in the access and assessment team.

Introduction

This book is written as a series of chapters comprised of academic work presented by experienced practitioners undertaking the Bournemouth University Post-Qualifying Child Care Specialist Award. Bournemouth University has been delivering a Post-Qualifying Child Care Award for the past five years and as a programme team we have been continually impressed by the high standard of work demonstrating practice of the highest quality.

The death of Baby Peter and subsequent inquiries highlight the need for radical change in social work education and training at both qualifying and post-qualifying level. In the report *The Protection of Children in England – A Progress Report* (2009) Lord Laming states:

> *The message of this report is clear; without the necessary specialist knowledge and skills social workers must not be allowed to practise in child protection.*

(Laming, 2009, p5)

The report makes many recommendations regarding social work education and training, including a national framework for continuous professional development for child care social workers. Lord Laming recommends:

> *As a first step, a post-graduate qualification in safeguarding children is needed that is practice-based, focusing on the key skills required for effective working with children and families and protecting children from harm. All children's social workers should be expected to complete this post-graduate qualification as soon as is practicable. It will need to be funded centrally and with protected study time made available.*

(Laming, 2009, p54)

We fully endorse these recommendations, particularly in terms of funding and protected study time, which is essential to enable students to step out of the highly pressured environment of social work practice and have time to enhance their specialist knowledge and skills, and to critically reflect.

The General Social Care Council introduced the curriculum for the Post-Qualifying Child Care Award and each chapter reflects one of the four main themes: Chapter 1 – Child development; Chapter 2 – Ecological factors; Chapter 3 – Legislation and social policy; and Chapter 4 – Managing the professional task. Each chapter includes two practice examples from different specialist areas and demonstrates key areas of knowledge identified in the National Occupational Standards for Child Care at a Post-Qualifying Level.

The revision of the Post-Qualifying Framework in 2007 broadened the curriculum and included more contemporary social work issues that reflected societal change. The work contained within this book highlights some of the challenges and dilemmas in safeguarding children at a practitioner level. It also demonstrates some of the complexities and diversity of the knowledge-base required within contemporary child care practice.

In spite of these pressures we have been amazed and inspired by the level of professionalism, commitment, energy and passion demonstrated by students undertaking the Post-Qualifying Specialist Child Care Award. This is reinforced by employers who comment on existing high standards of practice as well as students' enthusiasm for acquiring and incorporating new knowledge and learning into their work. There is also evidence of new knowledge and research being disseminated to the wider workforce as well as increased confidence in individual practitioners. This is set within the context of great media attention, often of a highly critical nature, and much political and public focus on the need to improve the safeguarding of children in the community.

As Lord Laming's report states:

> *Few careers are as demanding or rewarding as that of working with children, young people and their families.*

(Laming, 2009, p43)

Achieving a Post-Qualifying Social Work Award

This book will help you to meet the following Occupational Standards for Social Work

---

Unit A
Work directly with children and young people to achieve optimal outcomes

Unit B
Work with parents, families, carers and significant others to achieve optimal outcomes for children and young people

Unit C
Undertake and/or co-ordinate work the networks, communities and other agencies to achieve optimal outcomes for children and young people in need

Unit D
Undertake and/or co-ordinate the development of service policies and practices which optimise the life chances for all children and young people

Unit E
Take responsibility for the continuing professional development of self and others

If you are a registered social worker, this book will assist you to evidence post-registration training and learning. It relates to the national post-qualifying framework for social work education and training, especially the national criteria at the specialist level, in particular:

$\rightarrow$

---

i. Meet the relevant academic standards associated with social work at this level.

ii. Think critically about your own practice in the context of the GSCC codes of practice, national and international codes of professional ethics and the principles of diversity, equality and social inclusion in a wide range of situations, including those associated with inter-agency and inter-professional work.

iv. Draw on knowledge and understanding of service users' and carers' issues to actively contribute to strategies and practice which promote service users' and carers' rights and participation in line with the goals of choice, independence and empowerment.

v. Use reflection and critical analysis to continuously develop and improve your specialist practice, including your practice in inter-professional and inter-agency contexts, drawing systematically, accurately and appropriately on theories, models and relevant up-to-date research.

vii. Work effectively in a context of risk, uncertainty conflict and contradiction.

x. Effectively manage own work and demonstrate a capacity to plan for and respond to change in organisational, inter-organisational and team contexts.

Chapter 1

Child development

Contributors: Vanessa Bomphrey, Yvonne Mieville and Liz Reilly

ACHIEVING A POST-QUALIFYING SPECIALIST AWARD IN CHILD CARE

Knowledge of child and young person development is one of the common core of skills and knowledge for the children's workforce as well as a key area of knowledge identified in the National Occupational Standards at a post-qualifying level (DfES, 2005).

This chapter will help you to develop the required knowledge base.

Human growth and development
- Human growth and development including developmental milestones.
- Factors which promote a positive sense of self.
- Factors which ensure safe and effective care for children and young people, including secure attachment.
- The effects of insecure attachment and loss; the impact of all forms of abuse, violence, including domestic violence and other trauma have on the child/young person.

The Every Child Matters agenda introduced the government's aims for all children to:

- be healthy;
- stay safe;
- enjoy and achieve;
- make a positive contribution;
- achieve economic well-being;
(HMSO, 2003)

Policy and guidance take a developmental perspective to assessing the needs of children and providing universal services with the aim of all children being supported to reach their full potential in all significant areas of their lives. This requires that social workers and all those working with children have a foundation of evidence-based knowledge of child development.

The Framework for the Assessment of Children in Need and their Families (DoH, 2000), sets out a number of principles which should underpin all assessments including that they are:

- child-centred;

- rooted in child development.

It is important that practitioners have a comprehensive understanding of child development and all its stages in order to understand how other factors such as trauma, abuse and parenting impact on normal child development and have knowledge of how other factors such as culture, disability and environment must be taken into account when making an assessment from a developmental perspective.

In this chapter we will be including examples of how practitioners apply current knowledge of child development to their own practice including new research findings into brain development and current thinking around attachment and attachment disorders.

Key skills needed to develop an understanding of a child's developmental stage are observation and judgement. As part of our teaching of child development at a post-qualifying level, we offer students the opportunity to undertake child observations and at the end of the chapter we include some examples of how this has enabled them to reflect on new learning and the implications for their own practice.

The impact of early abuse and trauma on the developing infant brain

The following section is an extract from an assignment written by an education social worker undertaking the Post-Qualifying Specialist Child Care Award.

CASE STUDY

My first contact with Natasha, a white British child, was in Year 7 of secondary school. After a good primary school experience, Natasha was finding the transition to secondary school difficult and was refusing to attend. Natasha lived with her adoptive parents, also white British, who were reported to be at their wits' end with her behaviour at home, which included stealing, lying and aggressive behaviours towards her younger siblings. Natasha's parents explained that she had been removed from her birth parents at five months old, following physical abuse. She had then enjoyed a stable foster placement until the time of her adoptive placement. The adoptive family were increasingly frustrated and bewildered by Natasha's behaviour. They believed that they had offered a secure, loving home for nine years, the majority of Natasha's life, yet this love and stability had not been enough and her increasingly dangerous and destructive behaviours were becoming unmanageable within a family setting. They were overwhelmed and feared they would have to give her up.

Child development

Child development is a broad and diverse topic, and as Cicchetti and Rizley (1981, cited in Aldgate et al., 2006 p53) write, *the empirical study of child development is a perplexing scientific problem for which we have no ready answers or simple solutions.* There are many factors which impact upon the development of children, including genetic and environmental factors, as well as other theories about the stages of physical and cognitive development.

The following assignment extract focuses on the importance of attachment theory in the early development of infants and considers the impact of early abuse and trauma on attachment and on the developing infant brain. It will consider how these, together with separation and loss, can impact on subsequent development and relationships, and how practitioners can support carers and parents to increase resilience and lessen the long term effects of attachment disorders, abuse and loss. Education social workers are likely to be involved in the more complex issues around the education needs of children and young people, particularly in relation to school attendance.

A possible scenario might be to work with a child who is having difficulties in making the transition into secondary school. Many children and young people have complex histories which may include early trauma, abuse and issues around separation and loss. An example of this might be a child who has experienced some form of substitute care such as foster care, kinship care or adoption. It is very common that early experiences will impact on behaviour either at the time or indeed at a later date and it is therefore very important not to see the behaviour in isolation but to consider it within the context of the child's history.

Social workers can help parents and other service users understand and make sense of the current behaviour of children and young people by considering their past experiences and how these may have shaped their personality. Understanding a child's developmental stage and where behaviours come from can inform our practice in choosing appropriate intervention. It is worth bearing in mind, however, that while an understanding of background or a diagnosis of a particular condition can help us to choose interventions, it is only part of the story. The behaviour of the child does not change simply because we understand more about its cause; the stress for the child and carers remains the same. Diagnosis and understanding need to be followed up with appropriate therapy and support.

Nonetheless, theories of attachment can help professionals and carers to understand what babies and young children like Natasha need in their earliest months and years. They can help us to understand what some children have missed in their early development and to consider how, or even if, we can help them overcome any early damage.

> *Attachment theory involves the study of human relationships, especially early formative relationships. Further, the theory asserts that there is a biological imperative for infants to form attachments and that they exhibit attachment behaviours to promote attachment. In this sense attachment behaviour can be viewed as survival behaviour.*
>
> (Daniel et al., 2000, p14)

Bowlby identified the importance of a secure and loving relationship between mother and child from the earliest stages of babyhood in developing the child's sense of positive identity. Much of Bowlby's work focused only on the relationship with the mother. Later theorists have criticised this overemphasis on maternal care as simplistic, and have demonstrated that a primary attachment figure may be a father or other adult, and that other attachments from extended family or community members also contribute to healthy development (Smith et al., 2003). Theorists agree generally, however, that children need more than just *the physical necessities of life such as food and shelter: they also need human warmth and nurture if they are to grow up as functioning human beings* (Stainton Rogers, 2001, p211).

Human babies are born vulnerable and dependent upon their caregivers. Cairns (2002, p48) asserts that from birth, babies *show behaviours which actively contribute to (their) own survival*. These 'attachment behaviours' are designed to elicit a response from the caregiver to meet the baby's need. Behaviours might include crying or screaming, known as 'aversive' behaviours, eliciting an adult response to stop the behaviour by meeting the need, perhaps for food or a nappy change. The baby discovers 'attractive' behaviours, such as smiling, which will be enjoyed by a responsive carer and the baby. Later, the baby develops 'active' behaviours such as moving towards the carer to get attention and relieve stress.

Davenport (1989), reviewing some of the cross-cultural research, concluded that attachment behaviours in babies appear to be universal, and that babies will still attach to their primary carers even when much of the child-minding is not done by the parents, such as in a kibbutz. Aldgate et al. (2006) concur that attachment is universal but refer to further research suggesting that cultural and religious expectations of child behaviour may lead to differences in how attachment is demonstrated in behaviour. Practitioners need to be aware of these potential cultural differences and show sensitivity in the assessment process.

Howe et al. (1999, cited in Cairns, 2002, p52) describe how theories of attachment were tested and expanded upon in the work of Mary Ainsworth. Ainsworth noted three distinct patterns of attachment behaviour in infants, which she classified as secure attachment, insecure avoidant attachment and insecure anxious ambivalent attachment. Howe et al. (1999, cited in Cairns, 2002, p52) refer to the later work of Main and Soloman, who added a fourth response, disorganised attachment.

Following on from the work of Ainsworth, researchers have considered how the parent responds to the child's attachment behaviours. George and Soloman (1999, cited in Aldgate et al., 2006, p76) describe three groups of parents; those providing a secure base; those who reject and thereby deactivate the infant's attachment behaviours; and those who provide disorganised care by uncertain and helpless parenting.

Cairns (2002) asserts that a clear correlation has been found between the attachment style of the parent and the attachment pattern of the child. The attachment behaviours from the baby and the response from the carer are considered to be a two-way process, referred to as the cycle of attunement. Where the carer is responsive and available both adult and child move through a cycle of stress arousal, stress modulation and the pleasurable experience of stress relief.

The quality of these early attachment relationships is believed to affect significantly the quality of emotional relationships throughout a child's life and provides *a template of relationships or internal working model* (Howe, cited in Aldgate et al., 2006, p192).

Some children experience disordered attachments from birth. It is possible that a mother or other primary caregiver might have a limited ability to meet the child's basic needs, offering unpredictable care, which was the case for Natasha. There could be many reasons for this including their own experience of being parented, personality, chaotic home environment, addiction, mental health, domestic violence and other significant environmental factors. In these types of situation it is highly possible that the attunement necessary to secure healthy attachments may be absent.

Adults with unresolved attachment issues may find the attachment needs of their children triggering their own needs. An adult who has been unable to resolve these issues may have a damaged internal working model. They are unable to empathise with the needs of others, even infants, and may attribute unintended meaning to them. Thus a crying baby is perceived by the parent to be intentionally annoying them rather than signalling its need for comfort (Cairns, 2002).

This has implications for professionals assessing parenting capacity, where an understanding of the parent's attachment style can assist both in judging risk to the child and appropriate treatment for the parent. Indeed, Aldgate et al. (2006, p95) advise that assessments of parenting capacity should give *in-depth attention to assessing the sense caregivers have made of their earlier attachment experiences.*

ACTIVITY 1.1

Think of examples from your own casework where a greater understanding of a parent's own experience of being parented may have contributed to your understanding of the presenting problem and informed your intervention and provision of services.

Although for the purposes of this discussion we are particularly interested in theories of attachment in child development, it should be remembered that children and their carers are part of a wider society or system. The work of Bronfenbrenner (1989, cited in Daniel et al., p31) emphasises the importance of ecological factors in assessment, and that children should never be assessed in isolation from their environment. A holistic approach to assessment is required.

Early brain development

In recent years, alongside the development of attachment theories, there has been increasing research and understanding in neurophysiology and early brain development. Modern non-invasive techniques for scanning brains have given us significant additional insight into how early attachments seem to affect early brain development and for some children like Natasha may contribute to their ongoing difficulties. The significance of pathological, social and environmental impacts on development is becoming harder to refute.

We know that brain development begins in the womb. The developing foetus may be damaged by toxic substances such as drugs and alcohol, infectious diseases or nutrient deficiencies (Shonkoff, 2000).

Healthy babies are born with a brain which has the biological foundation to build neural connections according to the child's experiences. Babies with a secure attachment relationship are in the optimal condition for healthy brain development. Cairns (2002, p50) tells us that research shows *securely attached children develop bigger brains*.

Siegal (2007) refers to the science behind the developing brain, explaining that the brain changes in response to experience. It is experience, alongside genetic inheritance, that shapes the development of the area of the brain known as the cortex. Trauma damages both the hippocampus and the area behind the cortex; the middle prefrontal cortex. In the early years the majority of brain development affecting emotional development occurs in this prefrontal cortex. Siegal goes on to describe nine functions of the healthy prefrontal cortex, including attuned communication, emotional balance, empathy and insight. Attuned communication helps grow the prefrontal cortex, and can help adults grow what Siegal calls the *mindful brain*.

When very little is known about a child in terms of its history or genetic background, as may be the case for an adopted child, knowledge of attachment theory and research into early brain development is important in developing some understanding or explanation for presenting behaviours. The brain of a child who lacked an early, attuned relationship may be shaped very differently to his/her peers who have experienced healthy, securely attached relationships. They might well be working with a very different brain (Cairns, 2002). There is further research to suggest that abuse and trauma are additional factors in shaping early brain development, as well as laying down patterns of behaviour that are a physiological response to stress.

This can present a bleak picture to the professionals and carers working with children who have had poor early attachment experiences. Social workers assessing and gathering evidence on the parenting capacity of service users will expect to take some time to complete a full assessment. During this time, untold damage may be occurring in young brains. For example, adoptive parents might be fearful of the long-term consequences of the early attachment experiences.

However, there is reason to remain optimistic that the human brain has capacity for change. While Perry (2000, cited in Cairns, 2002, p51) considers from his research that injuries and developmental deficiencies from gestation up to eight months after birth cannot be reversed, there is increasing evidence that with the right therapy and protective factors, some of this early damage can be overcome. Shonkoff (2000, p217) suggests there is promising research regarding *the capacity of the brain to reorganise itself following highly depriving circumstances early in life*. Steinberg (2005, p73) refers to brain and cognitive development in adolescence, and suggests there is *emerging understanding of adolescence as a critical or sensitive period for a reorganisation of regulatory systems*, which is *fraught with both risks and opportunities*, but offers a further window of opportunity for change.

Cairns (2002) describes the physiological effects of trauma, and extreme danger. In normal circumstances, as we engage with our environment, all levels of the brain are activated. Under intense threat, the limbic system is activated instantly, flooding the body with stress hormones, and closing down higher-level functioning, such as reasoning. This is the primitive survival mechanism preparing the body for fight or flight. In small amounts, stress hormones are desirable in ensuring we are normally active, but Cairns states that in a traumatic situation the flooding of hormones represents an overdose of stress hormones and is actually toxic to some aspects of our functioning. Repeated trauma sets up patterns of behaviour which may have lifetime effects. Children who have been abused may be constantly hyper-aroused and on the alert for danger, but paradoxically very poor at assessing genuine risk. Minor triggers may initiate major survival responses, leading to disproportionate outbursts of rage or fear. This might well be the type of behaviour which causes a problem in a school setting or indeed elsewhere.

Lieberman (2007) asserts that unpredictable traumatic stress, including all forms of child abuse and witnessing domestic violence, affects every aspect of a child's development, culminating in pervasive behaviour problems. Lieberman also refers to anatomical and physical changes to the brain from traumatic stress, including less brain tissue and more fluid, higher levels of stress hormones in the brain, and a smaller frontal cortex.

Gibbons et al. (cited in Daniel et al., 2000, pp135–37) reported on a follow-up study of children on the child protection register, who had mostly been physically abused, which found significant behaviour differences as rated by parents and children compared to other non-abused children. These included restlessness, looking miserable and seeming solitary.

Vasta, Marshall and Miller (1999, cited in Aldgate et al., 2006, p192) suggest that from birth to 2 months, infants show indiscriminate responses to all people, and although recognising the primary caregiver within days, they do not show a marked preference. Between 2 and 7 months, they are more interested in the main carer and look to them for guidance in new situations. Between 9 and 24 months more focused attachment develops, with first a fear of strangers and then anxiety when separated from the caregiver.

If we take the example of an adopted child, removed from birth parents between 2 and 5 months and placed temporarily with foster carers, it is likely they might have some awareness of their situation and look for birth parents, but there may also be a lessening of anxiety as basic needs are met, allowing the child to show attachment behaviours and to build a cycle of attunement, forming a healthy bond with foster carers. If between 9 and 24 months the child is then placed with adoptive parents, this represents a further separation from primary caregivers and another loss.

Rutter (1981, cited in Aldgate et al., 2006, p193) suggests that *children between the ages of six months and four years are the most vulnerable to the worst aspects of separation because they have developed selective attachments and are laying the foundations of autonomy*.

Children between the ages of 2 and 5 years are at a stage of self-centredness. They have limited comprehension, with a tendency to concrete ideas. This self-centredness leads to 'magical thinking' – the belief that they are responsible for events around them. Therefore, they may develop the belief that they have been moved because they have been bad in some way. A child being placed with adoptive parents at a young age would not be able to understand verbal explanations about moving to a 'forever family', for example. Regression, bedwetting and 'testing out' behaviours are common in young children who experience loss or separation, whether this is through divorce, bereavement or social work interventions (Daniel et al., 2000).

Aldgate et al. (2006, p193) suggest ways in which practitioners can minimise the effects of separation on young children. These include *adequate preparation for (an) anticipated separation, warm, consistent substitute care,* maintaining *as many routines as possible, ongoing contact with the attachment figure* and that *any signs of self-blame are quickly picked up and defused*.

Many young people who are unable to live with their birth parents might have to cope with a number of further changes in carers before securing permanence. Littner (1975, cited in Daniel et al., 2000, p96) looks at the additional tasks for children placed apart from their birth families, which he identifies as a particularly vulnerable group. He refers to four forms of psychological scarring – *the freezing of personality development, excessive mistrust in people,* as *love is inevitably followed by loss, self-defeating behaviours* (driving carers to reject), and a *tendency in adulthood to repeat with own children the separation anxieties of the past*. Black and mixed-race children in the care system are especially vulnerable, needing additional support to enhance and nurture a positive racial identity.

Understandably adoptive parents can be optimistic that early trauma and separation may not be remembered, and therefore have no long-lasting effects. However, as I have discussed, poor early attachment and trauma appear to have lasting effects, leaving physical changes to the brain and patterns of behaviour which may be impervious to change. Separation and loss of foster carers as attachment figures may come at a critical developmental stage and cause lasting damage.

Understanding these effects can be the first step for carers and professionals in giving appropriate support. For parents, who may have been feeling a sense of failure that their love and care was not enough and that in some way, their parenting was inadequate, this knowledge may free them from their own sense of personal failure and allow them to ask for help.

Diagnosis of attachment disorders is complex and unlikely to be made in the child's early years. As an education social worker I have worked with children with a diagnosis of reactive attachment disorder made by child mental health professionals. Archer (2004, p205) refers to reactive attachment disorder as a *deeply distressed or distorted pattern of attachment, as a result of early traumatic experiences, which continue to influence . . . current social and emotional relationships.*

Hughes (2004) describes children with attachment difficulties as tending to have a variety of symptoms creating moderate or extreme difficulties in the major areas of their life. These symptoms affect basic biological regulation, modulation, integration, behavioural organisation and development of language. The lack of effective attunement leads to symptoms such as lack of joy, humour, eye contact, lack of guilt, and a lack of empathy. The child with an attachment disorder has excessive shame, which may lead to an excessive need to control, oppositional–defiant behaviour, intense negative affect, lies, excuses, dissociation and/or hyper-vigilance.

Similar symptoms may be exhibited by children who have other pervasive development disorders, particularly autistic spectrum disorders including Asperger's syndrome, and attention deficit hyperactivity disorder (ADHD) and attention deficit disorder (ADD). It is not possible to discuss these conditions in detail in this chapter. Briefly, however, children with autistic spectrum disorders show a *triad of impairment* used for diagnosis: social impairment, verbal impairment and repetitive/stereotyped activities (Gould, 1998).

Liekerman and Muter (2005) define ADHD and ADD as *a range of problem behaviours associated with poor attention span, including impulsiveness, restlessness, hyperactivity and inattentiveness preventing children from learning and socialising well.*

In my own practice, this overlap of symptoms means that it is important for me to have a wide-ranging overview of child development and disorders, and to consider all the possible variables during assessment. It is unlikely, however, that I or any one professional discipline will hold the entire range of knowledge needed for diagnosis and treatment, demonstrating the need for multi-agency partnerships. The Every Child Matters agenda, with a move towards multi-agency teams, and a *team around the child*, is recognition of how important it is to share information and knowledge in order to assist in assessing and managing risk and need (Department for Education and Science, 2004).

For the social worker in an education setting, one important aspect of the role can be to draw together the family and professionals in a multi-agency meeting, enabling us to review all the information we have, and to look at how and where support needs to be given.

Therapists working in the field of attachment difficulties recommend a specialist approach with parent and child, which offers reattunement opportunities as most effective, rather than individual work with the child, such as art therapy. Hughes (2004, pp302–3) gives 'Parenting guidelines for Attachment', including the development of an 'attitude' which is accepting, curious, empathic, loving and playful. He suggests that this specialist task of 'interactive repair' cannot be undertaken alone by the therapeutic carers but requires the personal and professional support of the community around the child.

Cairns (2002) agrees with the need for this approach, describing a four-step plan, including commitment of carers, personal support, professional supervision and working with others to build an environment to promote secure attachment. She describes the structured help needed as *therapeutic re-parenting* and argues that parenting insecure children is *often counterintuitive; carers have to learn how to parent the child with insecure attachments* (p115).

Perry (2006) states that the key to success is matching the correct therapeutic activities to the specific developmental stage and physiological needs of the traumatised child. Cairns also describes the difficulties of living with children with attachment issues and looks at the phenomena of transference and counter-transference. She notes how traumatised children *often seem to be surrounded by people who are extraordinarily angry or very sad*. Traumatised children who are unable to manage their own overwhelming feelings, have dissociated from them but are able to *survive by transferring to others in the social environment the now absent emotional experience* (Cairns, 2002, p115).

This emphasises the need for us as professionals to understand the intense feelings that abused children, including those with attachment disorders, can produce in their carers, if we are to be able to offer them non-judgemental support and care. Likewise, social workers working with families in difficult and challenging situations may commonly experience feelings of despair and 'stuckness' alongside the families and must look beyond their own feelings to the message that the emotional effect/counter-transference may give.

In my own practice, I have been able to transfer this knowledge to the education setting where these challenging behaviours in children may generate similarly strong feelings in education staff, who in spite of their often considerable teaching experience, may be unable to separate out the feelings generated in them personally from the underlying issues for the child. Individual attitudes and behaviours of staff can become uncompromising and unforgiving. They use discriminating language, and systems become oppressive. The traumatised child has unconsciously recreated the same abusive situation in school as at home.

Bromfield (2000) suggests that *Teachers' reactions can often sustain and strengthen undesirable behaviour* and cites Sweeney (1975), who wrote that *Behavioural research on conditioning affirms the Adlerian notion that what most adults do impulsively when they respond to misbehaviour is incorrect.*

Daniel et al., 1999 (cited in Aldgate et al., 2006, p153) refer to a positive school experience as a protective factor in the development of resilience, which should be encouraged. Jackson (2001, cited in Cairns, 2002, p156) also confirms that staying in mainstream school is a predictor for successful outcomes for children in public care. In addition, *A relationship with a significant adult outside a child's immediate family who offers consistent encouragement, and serves as a positive role model and advocate, is a factor associated with positive outcomes and the promotion of resilience* (Department of Health, 1996; Gilligan, 2001, cited in Aldgate et al., 2006).

An important part of my role in promoting resilience is to try to keep the educational experience positive for challenging pupils by offering insight to staff into the child's experiences and developmental stage. It is also to encourage tutors and teachers to maintain positive role models, and to ensure they receive the professional support and supervision needed to work with these desperately needy yet often rejecting young people.

My own practice has changed over the years as I have come to understand more about developmental and organic disorders, and in particular how these impact on a child's education. For a child whose non-school attendance and other challenging behaviours stem from insecure attachment, the main focus of the work to be done is specialist therapeutic work between child and parents.

My role will be one of partnership between child, parents, school and other professionals, looking for strengths in the systems surrounding the child. In practical terms for me, this is often in the school system. For example, it could be that we know that the child responds well to a particular learning support assistant who can meet them each morning or work in particular lessons. We may have learned that the child's moral development is delayed and he/she is unable to understand the social rules at lunchtimes, so we will not put them in the playground where they might fail, but in a secure nurture group, where they will succeed.

In conclusion, theories of early attachment and brain development can contribute to the understanding of long-term developmental difficulties for children and help us to choose appropriate interventions. Daniel et al. (2000, p300) urge us to remember that as *problems usually have complex causes and therefore complex or multi-faceted solutions*, so an *effective intervention will require a sufficiently comprehensive plan which embraces a number of approaches and which also attends to a lot of the little details*.

REFLECTION POINT

I undertook my initial social work training over 20 years ago, and my first marked assignment was on maternal deprivation. This assignment focused on a critical evaluation of my own practice using child development, attachment theories and current research in relation to a traumatised child. This assignment provided a really interesting and welcome opportunity to see how much more research has been done into early attachment, since I first studied the work of Bowlby and Rutter. In particular, modern brain-scanning techniques have allowed us to see the physical development of infant brains and the effects of early experiences on developing brains. This still-emerging research appears to support theories that positive parenting experiences grow healthy brains, while negative experiences can have long-lasting physical consequences for brain development, which in turn, affects emotional well-being.

For me, this helped to explain why children and young people might display emotionally disturbed behaviour many years after early trauma, and after years of good enough parenting by substitute carers. Some children cannot remember their early traumatic

→

experiences, and have received many years of stable, loving care. Their extreme behaviour seems inexplicable given their current circumstances, but once we begin to understand the potential impact of early experience on brain and emotional development, we can put these behaviours into context.

Importantly, for practitioners, there are also positive messages of hope from the research that the brain has the capacity to change and develop, and that specialist therapeutic work can overcome attachment disorders. In my own practice, I hope I have been able to use my own increased knowledge to enable parents and other education professionals, not only to understand more about early attachment, but to seek the specialist targeted support that some children need.

Child development and disability

This extract is taken from an assignment written by a social worker in a frontline children and families team. The student is reflecting on her knowledge of the stages of child development and applying this to children with a disability.

Defining and assessing child development is complex, particularly with the growing awareness and understanding of issues of disability and culture:

> *Development is defined as orderly and relatively enduring changes over time in physical and neurological structures, thought processes and behaviour. In the first 20 years of life these changes usually result in new, improved ways of reacting – that is, behaviour that is healthier, better organised, more complex, more stable, more competent or more efficient. We speak of advances from creeping to walking, from babbling to talking, or from concrete to abstract thinking as instances of development. In each such instance we judge the later appearing state to be a more adequate way of functioning than the earlier one.*

> Mussen et al. (1990, p4)

A lengthy definition, but one that appears to be the most appropriate. It seems to be accepted that children reach milestones, competencies, and usually in some sort of order, although this is not meant to imply a prescriptive, narrow 'normality', but more of a generalised framework. This is particularly relevant when considering issues of disability.

Certainly, the use of milestones can aid assessments with regard to obtaining the correct diagnosis and support, if required. However, once a disability has been recognised, milestones themselves should be carefully considered. This has been reinforced by Marchant (2001) who argues that:

> *Professionals should assess whether a child is developing in line with what would be expected of a child with similar impairments at a similar level of development (not necessarily age).*

> (p212)

Another group of children for whom milestones need to be a more fluid guide are those who are profoundly/terminally ill, a group often ignored. For them, Ben-Arieh (2002) argues that *children's development is being addressed in terms of their current well-being as well as their future well-becoming*. It is important to strike a balance between the recognition of any form of delay or difficulty, and the avoidance of any form of exclusion or stigmatisation. Such are the drawbacks of any attempt to 'normalise' behaviour or development (on all levels) in a chronological or sequential fashion. Such developmental progression can be misleading as children, whether or not they have a disability, will often miss a few steps, or move slowly or quickly through others. Meggitt and Sunderland (2000) argue that:

> children with special needs ... often seem to dance the developmental ladder ... in unusual and very uneven ways.

> (pvii)

Such developmental milestones could be argued to be a relatively simplistic measure, by themselves, of child development, as other factors can be seen to influence development (disability being one of them). Development progression has been the focus of a number of authors, including Fahlberg (1994), Meggitt and Sunderland (2000), and their work has provided important information regarding the expectations/predictions of milestones.

Practice issues – using child development and attachment theories

As practitioners working in complex situations we are often working with children with multiple difficulties and therefore a working knowledge of how to apply knowledge of child development to practice situations is essential.

An example might be a child suffering from both post-traumatic stress disorder (PTSD) and attachment disorder. When working in this type of situation the theoretical framework of knowledge needed will be much of what has previously been discussed but might include other approaches, including socio-genealogical connectedness, the impact of domestic violence, neglect, parental apathy, cultural issues.

Earlier in the chapter we looked at how stress and trauma affect brain development. In Sue Gerhardt's book *Why Love Matters* (2004) it is suggested that trauma, such as experiencing domestic violence, can affect the way a baby's brain physically develops. Gerhardt argues (convincingly) that a baby's brain is unfinished at birth, and that the quality (or lack of it) of the caregiver's attachment and the baby's emotional environment can have a significant impact on a developing brain. A secure attachment can lead to a secure internal working model, but if a baby seeks to have their needs met, and parents are unwilling/unable to meet these needs, the stress that this causes will disturb the baby's physical natural rhythms – the body's levels of cortisol rise, but the stress is not abated, and so cortisol levels flood the brain. Gerhardt explains that babies are born with the expectation of having stress managed for them, and are unable to deal with it alone. It has been recognised that *too much cortisol can affect the development of the orbitofrontal part of the prefrontal cortex* (Lyons et al., 2000a). This is a technical medical explanation, and Gerhardt's book discusses the effects of stress on a baby's brain in a similar vein.

A key point that Gerhardt makes is that stress experienced by a pregnant mother can lead to cortisol being passed to the baby in the womb via the placenta (Gitau et al., 2001a), which links into the nature–nurture debate.

It is not uncommon for social workers to be working with children and parents/carers where the mother may have experienced domestic violence during her pregnancy, leading to the unborn child experiencing stress in the womb and it is likely that this stress will continue after the birth. Again, it is not uncommon for a mother in this situation to use drugs or alcohol as a coping strategy, which may lead to emotional unavailability after the birth as well as having significant implications during gestation. I have worked, on occasion, with children who have suffered significant trauma and abuse in early childhood, leading to a diagnosis of Post Traumatic Stress Disorder (PTSD). It is a common symptom for children who have suffered in this way to experience flashbacks to traumatic memories.

Studies have demonstrated that a physical response by the amygdala, which is part of the limbic system and plays an important role in motivation, emotional behaviour and the development of memories, occurs in PTSD sufferers with the amygdala being in a constant hyperactive state (Liberzon et al., 1999). This can mean that the brain is initially flooded with cortisol, and then goes on to regulate itself to having a low baseline cortisol level in order to cope with the constant high levels of stress. This is in addition to remaining in a fearful state of mind. It is arguable that a brain scan can inform further health interventions, to aid recovery.

Trauma caused by domestic violence can be compounded by neglect of a child's basic needs. For some this may include emotional neglect, contributing to antisocial behaviour at home, school and in the community, poor self-esteem, poor educational attainment, emotional withdrawal and distance. Howe (2001) identifies four types of neglect. These include disorganised neglect, depressed/passive neglect, and emotional neglect and abuse. Children often experience chaos and disruption in the family home and parents may be preoccupied with their own needs and feelings, and be emotionally unavailable.

It could be supposed that the impact of both the biological processes in the brain, and the psychological stresses of trauma, neglect, and emotional abuse, have a significant impact on all aspects of a child's development.

A key part of a child's development is the development of identity. In casework where parents are separated, there may be much bitterness and dispute over contact arrangements and the situation may become particularly entrenched and difficult. We live in a diverse and multicultural society but nevertheless this does not always mean that it is a tolerant society. If we take as an example a child of mixed heritage from a maternal family of Romany Gypsy heritage and a paternal family from a traveller background, there is the potential for a great deal of culturally-based conflict between families which the child will be aware of and which will in many cases impact on the development of a positive identity in a child both in terms of their cultural identity and their sense of place within the family. If the child is aware of cultural views that Gypsy and traveller cultures should not mix, and that the travelling culture has less validity and worth than that of the Gypsy culture, it could arguably lead to the child feeling worthless.

Cultural norms, values and traditions interact with other factors to impact further on the child's development. For example, within both the Romany Gypsy and traveller communities, domestic violence can lead to particular difficulties, as *the only way to escape from a violent abuser may be to give up their cultural way of life as it is particularly difficult to disappear within the traveller networks* (Van Cleemput et al., undated).

When parents separate it could be suggested that the child suffers losses on two levels: the loss of a parent, however disorganised the attachment, and the loss of the part of his or her culture. The first could contribute to a deepening of the dis-organised attachment, the second to a lack of self-esteem.

In some disputed contact situations, such separations have *become a way of life* (Freund-lich, 1998). Owusu-Bempah (1995, p201) argues that the consequences and outcomes of such separations are variable, and the *socio-genealogical connectedness ... one of the possible psychosocial mechanisms mediating children's adjustment to separation or a loss of continuity*. He goes on to suggest that socio-genealogical connectedness is con-cerned with a child's perceptions of their place in their family's history, and the child's understandings of their parental biological and social backgrounds.

He further argues that a positive sense of family history and connectedness will con-tribute to a better sense of adjustment to family separation and the loss of a parent. A sense of connectedness does not necessarily require contact with an absent parent, but does require information presented in a positive way about the absent parent's family and social history. Other researchers have agreed with this argument – Derdeyn (1977) proposes that *knowledge about parents, even those who have abused their children, has a psychological value to a child*. Owusu-Bempah (2000) suggests that traumatised, abused children will attempt to sever connectedness with regard to the abusing parent.

As a practitioner it is important to have an understanding of the concept of socio-genealogical connectedness and of how to work to help develop a more positive sense of self, on a cultural and familial level.

> ## *REFLECTION POINT*
>
> *Child development is not just about having an awareness of developmental milestones. A sound knowledge and understanding of current thinking on attachment behaviours and how to work with these, including windows of opportunity to work therapeutically with children and young people, is crucial to good practice. Arguably one of the most exciting*
>
> →

REFLECTION POINT *continued*

areas of knowledge and research is how brain development is affected by experience of trauma and abuse as well as environmental factors. If a practitioner has an understanding of this it will inevitably inform and shape assessments, interventions and outcomes. For example, how stress experienced by the mother of an unborn child, will affect the brain development of her baby.

As a practitioner, you have a responsibility to ensure that you keep abreast of research findings.

Can you think of a practice situation where a greater understanding of how the developing brain is affected by stress might have led to a different approach to your intervention?

Child observation

As part of the learning experience in undertaking the Post-Qualifying Child Care Award at Bournemouth University, our students are asked to complete six direct observations of a pre-school child who is unknown to them. This requirement is greeted with mixed feelings as it represents a considerable amount of time and some feel that it is a luxury which is not open to them in practice. However, generally, after completion of the task, it proves to be one of the key areas of reflective learning. This may take the form of refreshing and realigning benchmarks for development; it may highlight the importance of realising how many interactions are missed by professionals working in busy child care settings or how the presence of professionals impacts on behaviours or as in the following extract, how personal and professional experiences can shape practice.

Reflective account of conducting a child observation as part of a Post-Qualifying Child Care Award

Observation style

I had plans to conduct my observations in a structured fashion, focusing on developmental milestones, to 'measure' a child against. I carried out child observations as part of my qualifying course, but have never worked directly with pre-school children since and although I now have two young children of my own, I have spent almost 15 years exclusively with young adults and so have little working knowledge of the pre-school to early adolescent years. In preparation, I dug out old notes on theories of child development and photocopied Sheridan's child development charts (DoH, 2000, pp23–8). As well as being groundwork for carrying out the observations, I felt this would be good preparation for my new post in a children and families intake team and would be undertaken on a study day rather than a work day and therefore there would be no pressure from work.

In the end, I had to cancel the first few observations and there was little of the structure that I had intended. The observation was written in free form, albeit with some tricks borrowed from the *Target the child method* as described in Fawcett (1996, p50) and slotted in before and after work, with notes being left in my bag for a week. Indeed, it reflected how my practice has developed in recent years – fitting visits in (or as a manager, fitting supervision in), with little time for either planning or reflection. While there was obvious learning about the normal parameters of child development for pre-school children, it was the reflective space in which the most profound learning came.

Doing not thinking

Skilled observers *learn how to be and not to do* (Fawcett, 1996, p4). This was the most important piece of learning for me, although the journey to 'being' or 'thinking' rather than 'doing' (Ruch, 2006) has only just begun again. I have become increasingly task-focused since qualifying in social work. Part of this may be to do with the competency-based framework I trained within, part about the practical nature of the job and part due to the focus on targets and performance indicators. In my personal life, time is ever squeezed by domestic commitments, reducing the time for anything but 'doing'. However, I think my choice of paths has in fact more to do with the sort of person I am and my preference for doing, perhaps as a distraction from thinking and being. Shapiro (1999) talks about coping styles as either 'engaged' or 'disengaged' and offers a framework for understanding how we cope with stressful and emotionally challenging situations. My own history of disadvantage and later social and employment choices, has exposed me to hostile, unpredictable and risky situations but little that fazes me. I would be considered resilient, practical and courageous, entering dangerous and emotionally-charged situations feeling calm and able to sort things out. However, I have begun to compare this with situations that I don't handle well; where I felt exposed and vulnerable and have also begun to question 'how' and 'why' I sort things out.

I can see links between my personal coping styles, professional practice and the way I approached the observations. With this in mind, I tried to 'be' in the later observations. I still had an agenda, finding it impossible not to look for things, rather than just *see* things, but at least I was also recognising and reflecting upon these cognitive, emotional and behavioural habits. I have tried to take this forward and sustain this in my new post, with supervisory help, although I suspect that supervision will still just have to 'fit in' and that the culture within this team might be towards 'doing' instead of 'thinking' and 'being'.

Remaining objective

I found this difficult on a number of levels. On the most obvious level, the child I was observing was female, aged three-and-a half, exactly between the ages of my own two daughters. I was making comparisons in my head to the only other two little girls who I know well. From *how would they perform the task she was doing?* Then more guiltily, *what would they be doing now? I miss my girls. Is this what it is like for them when they have to be looked after in a day care setting?* The daydream often ending in: *Oh I don't want to have to work…why do I do this job looking after other people's children when my own need me to be there for them?* It is not a thought I dwell on at work, but there are moments when the pain of it smacks the wind out of you and it happened more often within the context of an observation. Perhaps as mentioned above, it's about being out of that highly pressured, task-focused environment. Having space to ponder, think, reflect and look at things from the child's perspective invites or rather fails to completely suppress the emotional elements of the work.

Another difficulty that I experienced was when I'd see her struggling with a task as I'd want to help her. I could hardly keep in my seat when she failed to get her carer's attention, despite several polite and patient requests for help. I found myself being annoyed at her carers, a similar reaction I felt in my previous jobs with residential staff, foster carers and leaving care workers when I felt they had ignored obvious need. In *Leaving care work*, I saw the personal adviser role (DoH, 2000) as a much-needed champion for young people. We had a terrific team and mostly good foster carers but a minority were, at best, disinterested, preoccupied and lazy and at worst dispassionate, controlling and critical. Challenging this was probably the most stressful part of my job, having never once come across a young person I couldn't connect with. Again, I can see continuities running through my personal life, my professional practice and the child observation – a potential to overidentify with the child or young person and maybe interfere and rescue. I did manage to sit tight during the observations, and only intervened when asked or safety required it.

Conclusion

The observation felt like a luxury. I felt indulgent and guilty having time away from work and my own children to do it. But it was the reflection on these sorts of feelings that was most useful. It made me think about my own development as a child and my development as a social worker and manager over the last decade. The Child Care Award will be for me, like the observation, an opportunity to acquire new knowledge and also to think about how I process that knowledge, and how that in turn affects my practice.

FURTHER READING

Archer, C (2004) *First steps in parenting the child who hurts: Tiddlers and toddlers*. London: Jessica Kingsley Publishers.

Attwood, T (2007) *The complete guide to Asperger's syndrome*. London: Jessica Kingsley Publishers.

Jack, J and Owen, G (2003) *The missing side of the triangle: Assessing the importance of family and environmental factors in the lives of children*. Barkingside: Barnardo's.

Zigler, EF (2002) *First three years and beyond: Brain development and social policy*. New Haven, CT: Yale University Press. Available at: **http://site.ebrary.com/lib/bournemouth/DOC**

Chapter 2

Ecological factors

Contributors: Andrea Wilkinson, Janet Cheeseright and Mary Jones

ACHIEVING A POST-QUALIFYING SPECIALIST AWARD IN CHILD CARE

Knowledge of a child and young person's development in relation to their position within a family or caring network, as well as a wider social context, is one of the common core of skills and knowledge for the children's workforce as well as a key area of knowledge identified in the National Occupational Standards for Child Care at a post-qualifying level.

Ecological factors
- The range and diversity of social, family and community structures and partnerships in the UK.
- The role that the wider family, close friends, networks and communities play in supporting a child/ young person and their families.
- The influence of environmental, economic and social factors on the lives of children/young people and families.
- Main factors which can promote or diminish the appropriate response of the neighbourhood, networks and communities to the child/young person and their families and carers.
- Nature of participation. Partnership and empowerment and how to reduce social exclusion.
- Difference between communities of interest and geographical communities and the impact on healthy development.

The teaching and learning attached to this unit of the Specialist Child Care Award are very much linked to the assessment process and in particular to an ecological model of assessment (Bronfenbrenner, 1979). Students undertaking this specialist award work in diverse settings and work to a variety of assessment frameworks including the youth offending, asset framework, Form F fostering assessments and initial and core assessments using the Framework for the Assessment of Children in Need and their Families (2000). However, these frameworks are all based on an ecological model which is essentially a systems model that looks at the child within the context of the family and wider networks, considering the influences and interconnectedness of the different systems and the impact on child development, welfare and safety.

Students are asked to critique the ecological model of assessment within the context of their own practice, considering the impact of policy and guidance at both an organisational and a national level.

There is often some resistance from experienced practitioners, to what they regard as revisiting areas of knowledge with which they are already familiar. However, it becomes apparent that in practice, they often have a very narrow focus on the networks with which the child has direct involvement and frequently ask what is the point of considering wider, more structural factors such as the impact of poverty, homelessness, social exclusion and wider societal, cultural and political factors, when they have no power to effect change in these areas? However, it is very encouraging that when given the opportunity to step back from practice and undertake their own research, they are able to broaden their knowledge and demonstrate their skills in critical analysis and recognise the importance of assessing child development and outcomes within a much wider, evidence-based and theoretical context.

Assessment issues for children with a disability

The following section is taken from an assignment written by a social worker working in a community support team for Children with Disabilities and evidences working to the following GSCC Specialist Standards.

Specialist level skills and knowledge requirements
ii. Application of assessment models and frameworks (including the selective use of the common assessment framework) to assessment needs, including additional complex needs associated with:
The physical and mental health needs of children:
a. and young people (including a knowledge and understanding of how to use the services that exist to meet those needs).
c. The needs of children and young people with physical impairments and/or learning difficulties (including a knowledge and understanding of how to use the services which exist to meet those needs).

(General Social Care Council, 2005, p11)

The Framework for the Assessment of Children in Need and their Families (DoH, 2000)

The Framework for the Assessment of Children in Need and their Families (DoH, 2000) is based on an ecological model of assessment, which provides a systematic way of analysing, understanding and recording what is happening to children and young people within their families and the wider context of the community in which they live (Horwath, 2002). Children's needs are assessed according to the three domains of the framework: child's developmental needs, parenting capacity and wider family and environmental factors. The assessment framework embraces the notion that the child, the child's family and the environments in which they live are in a constant process of reciprocal interaction (Jack and Gill, 2003).

The Framework for the Assessment of Children in Need and their Families was introduced in 2000 as part of the government's Quality Protects programme, which was part of the agenda to modernise the management of children's services (Calder and Hackett, 2003). The underpinning principles of the assessment framework emphasise that assessments should be child-centred, rooted in child development, and that professionals should recognise and work with diversity, building on family strengths as well as recognising difficulties (Horwath, 2002). Part of the critique that is levelled at the assessment framework is that practitioners may fail to adopt a fully ecological approach as they do not always pay equal attention to all three domains, which can result in a distorted or lop-sided assessment where the primary focus may be on the developmental needs of the child without proper attention being given to other relevant areas. Some argue that the assessment becomes motivated by workers focusing on the completion of recording within set timescales (Horwath, 2002, p199).

This discussion uses a practice example to consider the relevance of undertaking an assessment from an ecological perspective, which examines parenting capacity, the influence of family and environmental factors and the impact on a child's developmental needs and the interaction between these domains. For a social worker working in a local authority with disabled children and their families, the Framework for the Assessment of Children in Need and their Families (DoH, 2000) informs and underpins practice. However, it is only fairly recently that this assessment tool has been available for disabled children, which embraces all three domains of the assessment framework. Until recently, in some local authorities, disabled children had their needs met via the Community Care structure, where the main focus was on adult service users. The organisational context in which social work takes place influences the assessment process and it is important to question how far disabled children have been valued within this adult framework and how this has affected what happens for them (Calder and Hackett, 2003). It could be argued that placing responsibility for disabled children in teams that are concerned with adult service users has inevitably meant marginalisation of the former.

The legal and policy context

Practitioners working with disabled children are working within a complex legislative framework with requirements for a range of assessments from a number of pieces of legislation, including the Carers (Recognition and Services) Act 1995, Carers and Disabled Children Act 2000, The Community Care (Direct Payments Act) 1996 and the NHS and Community Care Act 1990 as well as child care legislation (Calder and Hackett, 2003). Conflicts of interest may arise between the focus of assessment on the child's needs and the focus of carers' legislation on the carers' needs (Calder and Hackett 2003). Historically assessments with disabled children have focused on the parents' support needs. It is argued that this is a practice which focuses negatively on the child as there is a tendency to over-empathise with the parents and carers (Calder and Hackett, 2003).

David is a 14-year-old boy with a learning disability who had been labelled as having challenging behaviour. David had been educated in a residential school out of county, returning to his mother in the school holidays. He was desperately unhappy at this school and was moved to a residential one in his locality. A referral was made to social services as he kept absconding from his new school.

Comment

It became apparent from the professionals already involved that the focus of the assessment was on David's behaviour. It could be argued that one of the major contributing factors to the continuing oppression of disabled children is the use of the medical model of disability as a basis of intervention. Oliver (1996) argues that the medical model:

> *Locates the 'problem' of disability within the individual and . . . sees the causes of this problem as stemming from the functional limitations or psychological losses which are assumed to arise from disability.*

(p32)

Mitler (1994) and Dale (1999) (cited in Cooper, 2000, p249) argue that by professionals working to a pathological model, they emphasise the negative characteristics of children's impairments, which become dominated by the belief that the family is disabled by the child's condition and that all family problems are associated to abnormality in the child. While on this matter it is important to stress that even the Children Act 1989 can be criticised for offering a definition of disability which embraces the language of the medical model.

> *A child is disabled if he is blind, deaf, dumb or suffers from mental disorder of any kind or is substantially and permanently handicapped by illness, injury or congenital deformity or such other disability as may be described.*

(Cooper, 2000, p243)

Middleton (1996) argues that the wording of this gives scope for interpretation and justification for widening or restricting access to services. In my opinion, using categories of disability means that certain children may slip through the net of eligibility and not receive a service at all.

ACTIVITY **2.1**

Think of ways in which the medical model of disability might impact on outcomes for a child in respect of the three domains of the assessment framework.
- *child's developmental needs;*
- *parenting capacity;*
- *family and environmental factors.*

The Social Services Inspectorate report (1994), *Services to Disabled Children and their Families* (cited in Beresford et al., 1996), highlighted that services for disabled children were likely to be eroded due to the increasing pressure of child protection work. It would seem that social work has divided itself into areas which it considers to be high and low status and this has inevitably compounded the discrimination towards disabled children. Griffiths (2002) argues that social work with disabled children and people has never been considered high-priority work. As Thompson (1997) reasons:

> It is 'subsumed within medical discourse and seen as a paramedical under-taking somewhat distanced from mainstream social work . . . It is thus given low status, low levels of funding and relatively little attention in terms of research and professional development.

> (p106)

It can be argued that many families who find themselves ensnared in the child protection system may have experienced multiple disadvantages and needed help at an earlier stage to help them confront their difficulties, before issues with parenting spiral into abuse (Calder and Hackett, 2003). My social work role with disabled children and their families is one that focuses mainly on 'family support', provided to children in 'need' under section 17 of the Children Act 1989. I believe that this model of support prevents many cases from entering the child protection arena. Although I understand that child protection systems are under-resourced and understaffed (Calder and Hackett, 2003), this is echoed in teams working with children with disabilities. I believe that recognition is not given to the work and support that disability teams provide and this is reflected for example, in heavier caseloads and pay scales. It would seem that systematic discrimination is therefore implicit within the organisational structure of services for disabled children. As an individual worker I practise in a non-discriminatory manner but as Chinnery (1990) argues:

> Individual workers may well act in non-disabling ways, but the structure of services which reaches far beyond that which is visible to disabled users, militates actively and very effectively against individual efforts to promote a helpful, non-disabling client-orientated service.

> (p53)

A core assessment was undertaken with the family in order to ascertain the needs of David and his mother's capacity to respond to his needs within the context of their wider family and community (Gray, 2003). A core assessment is conducted when a child's' needs must be comprehensively understood, and is used to see if the child can be safeguarded against harm (DfES, 2003). The assessment framework sets down very rigid timescales for the process of assessment, with a maximum timescale of 35 working days (Gray, 2003). Research shows that in 2003 only 56 per cent of core assessments were completed within the set timescale (DfES, 2003). Thorough assessments take time as the process is an ongoing event to ensure that all the relevant information has been collated (Coulshed and Orme, 1998). These timescales contradict the principle that assessment is an ongoing process rather than a one-off event, and could result in practice where families are being 'done to' rather than 'engaged with' (Calder and Hackett, 2003).

Ecological factors

It is argued that a distorted or lop-sided form of assessment can occur if professionals do not pay equal attention to the three dimensions of the assessment framework. Distorted assessments can lead to oppressive practice (Horwath, 2002). For example, I felt that some of David's needs had become marginalised due to his behaviour, as professionals had over-empathised with his mother and lost their focus on him as the child. It is recognised that interventions resulting in this type of assessment ignore parenting issues and the parenting environment (Horwath, 2002). 'Good-enough' parenting may be measured in terms of parents doing their best even if they fail to meet their child's needs (Reder et al., 1993 cited in Horwath, 2002, p200). An individual's capacity to parent a child may fluctuate due to a range of factors and influences, which may make it more or less likely that the child reaches its developmental outcomes (Calder and Hackett, 2003).

Research carried out in a sample of 200 families by Quine and Pahl (1995) into the causes of stress in families with a severely disabled child found the most stressful factors to be: behaviour problems in the child, night time disturbance, social isolation of the mother, adversity in the family, multiplicity of impairments, problems with child's appearance, and financial strain. In this case a number of these factors could be related to the family. However, on reflection I found that David's mother saw his behaviour as the main problem and she had difficulty recognising other factors which may have impacted on her own parenting capacity (Horwath, 2001).

It has been shown that social isolation is a clear risk factor for poorer health, and conversely, social integration is strongly associated with good health and psychosocial well-being (Blaxter, 1990, cited in Jack, 2000, p707). Social isolation was a factor that was affecting David's mother and this was intensified by her depression. Bion (1962, cited in Hindle, 1998, p264) suggests that if a parent or main carer with mental health difficulties is preoccupied or emotionally unavailable, it is then hard for the child to have a sustained experience of feeling contained and having their distress and confusion understood. A study by Sheppard (1997, cited in Calder and Hackett, 2003) found 33 per cent of mothers on social work caseloads to be moderately or severely depressed. David's mother had endured severe post-natal depression; she was also a single parent, and these are just two of the factors which are likely to pose considerable risks to the child (Calder and Hackett, 2003). On reflection it was apparent that David's mother was so preoccupied with her own distress and unhappiness that she was not physically or psychologically available to David. Research shows that in neglecting families, this often seems to be the case (Calder and Hackett, 2003). As Beresford (1994) identified, some emotional coping mechanisms such as over-reliance on tranquillisers or alcohol can prove harmful, leading to avoidance rather than a resolution of stress. David's mother had been on antidepressants for the previous 14 years. Research by Sheppard (1994, cited in Jack, 1997, p110) indicates that maternal depression is associated with a variety of child development problems including emotional disorders, behavioural disturbance and language delay.

It is acknowledged that poverty is one of the main factors in social exclusion and it is estimated that 55 per cent of families with disabled children are on a low incomes (DoH, 2004). David's mother was a single parent and research indicates that these parents fare worst, with 75 per cent relying on state benefits (Office of Population Censuses and Surveys (OPCS), 1989, cited in Mutch, 2003).

Comment

The government does not have any current information on numbers of disabled children and still relies on the figure of 360,000 cited in the 1989 OPCS report (Child Poverty Action Group, 2009).

The strains imposed by lack of money exacerbate an already stressful situation. It is estimated that the annual cost of raising a disabled child is three times greater than that for a non-disabled child (DoH, 2004). The financial strains of daily caring and often the inability to take on part-time employment may result in isolation and increased stress (Mutch, 2003). Another source of stress is the complexity of the benefit system. Research has indicated that there is a significant underapplication for Disability Living Allowance, with the most disadvantaged families from minority ethnic backgrounds being the least likely to apply and receive this benefit (DoH, 2004). I have worked with several families who dread the renewal application for Disability Living Allowance because it can take several hours to complete, and the focus is on all the negative things that their disabled child is not able to do compared with a non-disabled child. Middleton (1996) argues how services are disabling when service users have to exaggerate their impairments and the restrictions they face in order to get a service at all.

Single-parent families generally have lower incomes and therefore less access to such potentially stress-reducing factors as social outings, shared care, good housing (Mutch 2003). They may also lack a sharer of both physical and emotional problems – someone to take the strain when care demands become taxing. A survey by Quine and Pahl (1985) found that mothers in two-parent families had much lower malaise scores than mothers who were bringing up children on their own (p511). Significantly, even a marriage or partnership that was perceived as not supportive appeared to be less stressful than single parenthood. Mothers whose marriage offered no emotional support were less stressed than single mothers (Beresford, 1993). Perhaps this may be accounted for by the fact that this group were possibly receiving physical or financial support, or that shared responsibility may have relieved some of the pressure. Mothers of disabled children are less likely to be in paid employment due to the care demands placed on them (DoH, 2004). McConachie and Mitchell (1995, cited in Mutch, 2003, p21) acknowledge that although fathers are generally assumed today to have more involvement in parenting, most services are still constructed with predominantly the mother in mind. In my experience many fathers play a fundamental role in the family when a child is disabled; however, research indicates that many feel excluded from particular aspects of their child's care (DoH, 2004). Although David's father had not had contact with him since his birth, it is important to acknowledge that fathers either by their absence or presence can impact on the child (Horwath, 2002).

RESEARCH SUMMARY

SCIE research briefing 18: Being a father to a child with disabilities: issues and what helps. *Available at:* **http://www.scie.org.uk/publications/briefings/briefing18/references.asp** *(Accessed 14 April 2009)*

This research briefing includes some key messages.

- *Fathers of disabled children are fathers first, and fathers of a disabled child second. Many of the issues faced by fathers of disabled children are the same as those of fathers of non-disabled children.*

- *Fathers and mothers of disabled children have many of the same needs and concerns, but there can also be real differences in how they respond to their child's condition, what they do to cope, and what they find helpful.*

- *Fathers can be greatly affected emotionally by a child's disability, impairment or illness.*

- *Fathers want information about their child's condition and development, what can be done to help, and what services are available to help their child and the family as a whole.*

- *Fathers tend to rely heavily on their partners for emotional support.*

- *Fathers want someone to talk to from outside the family about their worries and concerns, but are not very good at seeking this type of help or support. They also prefer groups made up of men only because they feel more able to be open in such an environment.*

- *The needs of fathers can be missed by services, which tend to focus on support for the child and mother.*

- *Going to work is a common coping strategy of fathers and important for identity and self-esteem. Fathers want flexibility from employers and services so that they can respond to the needs of their children, attend appointments and be involved in the decisions and care relating to their child.*

Cassel (1976, cited in Jack, 1997, p109) highlights the importance of strengthening personal support networks as a means of preventing illness, rather than trying to reduce an individual's exposure to stressors. Social support networks can influence the quality of family life and outcomes for children. Informal support networks may consist of immediate extended family, friends and neighbours (Mutch, 2003). Research in the field of psychology has shown informal social support to be an essential coping resource (Venters, 1981; Quittner et al., 1990). However, it is important to stress that network relationships can be sources of both support and stress, and it is therefore important to examine whether they are liable to assist or undermine family functioning (Jack, 2000). This was the case with David and his mother, because they did not have a positive family network. Working from an ecological perspective it was possible to establish a clear picture of the stresses experienced by the family and what supportive resources were available to them (Jack, 2000). The extent to which supportive networks are utilised will be dependent to a large extent on the parents' own personality and temperament. Sloper and Turner (1993) state extroversion … suggests a resource factor specific to adaptation to the child (p182). They conclude that mothers who do not utilise informal support … tended to be at greater risk (p183). As informal networks were lacking, it was identified that David's mother needed emotional support, help with social integration and practical support; these are defined as the most important and frequently identified dimensions (Cutrona and Russell, 1990, cited in Jack, 1997, p110).

It is acknowledged that parents who neglect have many unmet needs of their own (Stevenson, 1998; Stone, 1998, cited in Calder et al., 2003, p220).

A formal support package was constructed for David's mother which consisted of a referral for therapeutic counselling, a community support worker to work as a befriender by helping her to access community resources, and domestic support in the home. There was also the support of a multi-agency team which included a social worker from the child protection team, a social worker for disabled children, education and health professionals. The aim of this support package was not to promote dependency but to provide support to the mother with her own unmet needs, which in turn would impact on her parenting, and help to extend her networks. Evidence shows that where there is a failure by professionals to provide adequate support in the early stages of intervention, this increases the chances of the child becoming looked after (Barn, 1998, cited in DoH, 2000, p64).

As David's mother showed a willingness to work in partnership towards these identified goals, this was recognised as a parental strength (O'Hagan, 1997). Building on family strengths as well as identifying limitations is another key principle of the assessment framework. However, it is argued that social work practice with black families has frequently failed to recognise and build on the strengths of black families, and has therefore problematised them (DoH, 2000). As Dominelli (1997) points out, white supremacist ideology is deeply rooted in social work practice; practitioners therefore need to be aware of judging black child-rearing methods as inferior to white ones. Although David's mother's needs were addressed, I realised that his needs as the child must have priority, as it is not fair for children to wait indefinitely for their parents to get their lives sorted out (Jack and Gill, 2003).

It can be argued that disabled children and their families commonly experience exclusion from ordinary child and family activities, as well as some mainstream and community services. Families from minority ethnic and asylum-seeking families have exceptional difficulties in obtaining services as there are higher levels of exclusion, unmet need and reduced levels of services than for white families (DoH, 2004). A study by Shah (1995, cited in Cooper, 2000, p249) records a range of difficulties experienced by Asian families at the hands of service providers; this includes stereotypical assumptions which are held by white practitioners, attitude and language barriers, which all result in service responses which are deeply discriminatory. Parallels of oppression can be drawn between the cumulative effects from race and disability in a society that is dominated by white and non-disabled norms (Begum, 1991, cited in DoH, 2000).

Having established that intervention based on the medical model is both oppressive and potentially damaging to the disabled child's self-esteem, it is important to stress that my practice is influenced by the social model of disability which places disability in the wider context of society. An individual is disabled, not by the impairment, but by *the failure of society to take account of and organise around difference* (Dowling and Dolan, 2001, p23). Article 23 of the United Nations Convention on the Rights of the Child acknowledges that disabled children have the right to achieve the fullest possible social integration and development (Cooper, 2000). On reflection I have to question how far this article is being adhered to when disabled children are still being sent to schools miles out of their geographical area. Lack of social integration and social isolation were factors which affected David. He had not attended the school that was in his locality, but one that was segregated, some distance from his home. Therefore he had no friends at home, and what friendship he did have was confined to limited family members. Middleton (1996, cited in Cooper, 2000, p243) argues that exclusion both results in and reinforces the stigma attached to people perceived as different through their impairments. Such attitudes explain why disabled people are located in segregated resources where they are denied the opportunity for full citizenship (Hirst and Baldwin, 1994, cited in Cooper, p243).

In my experience I have to agree that patterns of care are tolerated for disabled children that would not be tolerated for non-disabled children (Horwath, 2001). Many disabled children have their care provided in multiple settings such as hospitals, residential schools, with link families and at various respite centres (Griffiths, 2002). Children living away from home are vulnerable to risk factors such as abuse, over-medication, lack of emotional support, poor feeding and toileting arrangements (Cooper 2000). Little is known about the experience of disabled children at residential schools from their own point of view. Research carried out by Abbot et al. (2001, p72) which examined the experiences of 32 children in specialist residential schools found that care practices varied from excellent and warm, committed and engaged to very dehumanising, where little respect was shown for the children concerned. The research indicated that these children had little contact with the wider community during term time; some schools were good at maintaining parental contact; however, some parents had difficulty in keeping contact. From my own experience, disabled children attending residential schools are very isolated and their families receive minimal support from the local authority to maintain this contact.

Finkelstein and Stuart (cited in Hales, 1996) argue the topic of special education and mention how able-bodied adults tend to form the policies of education for both able-bodied and disabled children. As a result the educational needs of disabled children are framed as not just different, but special. Finkelstein and Stuart reason that the label of needing special attention constitutes a problem that can impact negatively on a disabled child's identity. This was the case for David as he had begun to query why he was being sent to a different school to that of other children. An important pointer for social work practice concerning identity is to question what messages the child is receiving about what it means to be disabled (DoH, 2000). On reflection it was apparent that David had received negative messages about being disabled and had internalised them. This had affected his sense of value and worth (DoH, 2000). In order for disabled children to counteract negative stereotypes they need a positive internal model of disabled identity (DoH, 2000).

The Department of Health (1991a, para. 6.7, cited in Cooper, 2000, p241) states that disabled children's views are important and should be actively sought. David expressed that he did not want to stay overnight at the residential school but to be at home. Within the ecological model it is important for social workers to place a strong emphasis on a phenomenological approach where the individual's own perceptions of their own circumstances is a central feature to the assessment and informs further action (Stepney and Ford, 2000). The placement choice of most young people and children is with their family (Korensen, 1993). It would seem that the emphasis on disabled children's health and educational provision has frequently been provided in institutional settings and this has therefore obscured their social care needs (Cooper, 2000). Listening to the child is therefore crucial; and this leads me to reflect on one of the points raised by Lord Laming in relation to contact with Victoria Climbié. He was extremely critical that she had never been spoken to on her own (Rustin, 2004). Privacy might have allowed her to convey more of the truth and might even have prevented her death.

The impact of disabled children using specialist services that are not provided in the communities in which they live may result in them not having opportunities for play and socialisation with non-disabled children (DoH, 2004). When the opportunity does arise, many disabled children find these interactions difficult (DoH, 2004). This was something that could be related to David, for although he had tried to access play facilities in his locality he had been unable to access them because of the threat of being verbally and physically bullied (Jack and Gill, 2003). Bullying can have very serious consequences as Kochenderfer and Ladd (1996, cited in Smith, et al., 2003, p165) found in a study of 5–6-year-olds, continual victimisation can lead to isolation, school avoidance, low self-esteem and self-confidence, and a lack of close friends at school. Davis and Watson (2001) found that disabled children have one thing in common: as one of the children expressed when asked what disability meant, *we all get picked on*. The children spoke of being bullied, which involved name-calling such as 'spastic' or 'deaf bastard', to being hit and kicked and excluded from peer groups. In the lives of minority ethnic children, racism and racial bullying are also commonplace. A small study by Begum (1992, cited in DoH, 2000, p57) on Asian disabled people and their carers showed that they had suffered from dual oppression where they had encountered both racist and disability discrimination.

As support was in place for David's mother to aid her in her parenting and her own personal unmet needs, David's wish to live with her was fulfilled. It is important that children have their wishes and feelings taken into account in order to inform the decisions that are executed (DoH, 2000). David needed this sense of belonging, as it gave him a sense of security. Children's relationships with their parents are crucial to their sense of well-being and the impact on later personal relationships (Andersson, 2004). This is a dominant message in attachment theory which is essential for understanding a child's reaction to separation and placement in foster or residential care (Andersson 2004). Had David's mother been reluctant to work in partnership with the department, I would not have felt reassured that his needs were being responded to at home. Therefore it might have been necessary to find David an alternative placement with substitute carers as there was no suitable extended family.

If a child needs to be removed from their home, placement with relatives must be explored as this may help to alleviate the child's trauma and promote their identity (Fahlberg, 1985). A child's identity is more likely to be preserved when the foster carers share the same ethnicity and culture as the child (Thomas and Pierson, 1995). Continuity and stability are essential for looked-after children as Kendrick's study (1985, cited in Holland et al., 2004, p29) suggests; one-third of children have experienced three moves or more within the care system in a year.

Responsibility for the child's welfare does not only lie with the parent and families but also with society and the communities in which they live (O'Hagan, 2001). As David had no contact with other young people in the community it was important to enhance his resilience (Kelly and Gilligan, 2002). Activities such as attending a local youth club and a gym with a support worker were arranged. Spare-time activities are said to help promote a child's sense of belonging, and to enhance their self-esteem and efficacy (Horwath, 2001).

The ecological approach to assessment takes into account a wide range of factors encouraging a worker to regard all domains of a family's circumstances, including those at individual, family, community and societal levels (Stepney and Ford, 2000). It embraces an anti-discriminatory stance as it helps to recognise structural causes of oppression such as the fundamental role played by poverty, and how this impacts on the health and development of children, which may impact negatively on family functioning (Jack, 2000). Looking at this case study and my work generally from an ecological perspective has highlighted that structural discrimination has been endemic in organisations in respect of meeting the needs of disabled children. This is demonstrated by the fact that it is only relatively recently that they stopped having their needs met in an adult social care setting. On reflection, it has been difficult for assessments to be truly child-centred, when the environment you work in is targeted towards the needs of adults rather than children. The disabled children that I work with now have their needs met through a children's service which is inclusive to the needs of all children and hopefully this will help to ensure that disabled children's lives are enhanced. An ecological approach recognises the barriers to disabled children's participation in accessing inclusive mainstream services, such as education and leisure activities. It strengthens families' support networks both informal and formal and encourages the social interaction between members of the community. This approach helps the worker comprehend how a family's condition can be intensified by issues relating to social support, social capital and social–economic disadvantage which can impact on the family's environment, sense of community, parenting capacity and their access to resources. It is therefore essential for practitioners to incorporate the ecological approach in their daily practice as it helps to determine the most appropriate level of intervention (Stepney and Ford, 2000).

Working with unaccompanied asylum-seeking children and young people

The following section is taken from an assignment written by a student working in a Youth Offending team and evidences working to the following GSCC Specialist Standards.

Specialist level skills and knowledge requirements

ii. Application of assessment models and frameworks (including the selective use of the common assessment framework) to assessment needs, including additional complex needs associated with:

d. The needs of young people involved with the youth and family justice systems (including a knowledge and understanding of how to use the services that exist to meet those needs).

e. The needs of children and young people in asylum-seeking families and unaccompanied asylum-seeking children (including a knowledge and understanding of how to use the services that exist to meet those needs).

(General Social Care Council, 2005, p11)

This case study is based on an assessment undertaken in my practice and aims to critically assess the influence of environmental factors on developmental outcomes for children and young people. It discusses ecological models of assessment and examines the potential and limitation of the social work role. The case study being presented relates to a young person who is an unaccompanied asylum seeker. The implications for this client group in particular is examined within an ecological perspective. The material submitted has been anonymised and where names do appear they have been changed.

CASE STUDY

Ehsan was referred to the Youth Offending Service by the Crown Court, having been found guilty of wounding with a knife. This offence had occurred nine months before the trial. The Court had requested that a Pre-Sentence Report be prepared and had indicated that all sentencing options were being considered, including that of custody. At the time Ehsan committed the offence he was 15 years old and had been living in the UK for three months. He had travelled cross-continent in the back of a lorry from his home in Afghanistan. Upon arrival he was unable to speak English and was illiterate in his own language. When he left home his father had been missing for some time, and since his arrival in the UK he had lost all contact with his family. As an unaccompanied minor he had been granted discretionary leave to remain in the UK until his eighteenth birthday (Immigration and Asylum Act 1999). He was defined as a child in need and was accommodated in foster care under section 20 of the Children Act 1989.

The Home Office has targets to reduce the number of successful asylum claims (Fekete, 2005). The tension between this policy and the principles of promoting equality and justice within minority ethnic communities places social workers at the vanguard of the current debate on asylum seekers and whether their continued stay is to be judged 'not conducive to the public good'. The concept of an asylum seeker being 'not conducive' to the public good is used as justification for deportation (Montgomery, 2004). While Ehsan was not at risk of immediate deportation, the fact that he had been convicted of a serious offence in the UK will impact upon the Home Office decision when he reaches 18. Although the state of affairs in Afghanistan is constantly featured in the media, I was aware of the need to gain a greater insight into Ehsan's experience, which led me to more in-depth reading about the political/ cultural/religious divisions within this country. This was informed by general systems theory, which conceives of the entire social world as interdependent parts of a much greater whole (Stein, 1974) and the view that people are not thought of as isolated individuals but as elements in a social system which includes but also transcends them. The ecological approach to assessment is derived from general systems theory.

Ecological systems theory, put forward by Bronfenbrenner, suggests that human development is not influenced by one factor but by a whole constellation of factors (Paquette and Ryan, 2004). Children are influenced primarily by their families but they grow up in expanding environments in which they are influenced by peers, school and the community in which they live. The main dimensions of a child's developmental needs are represented in the Framework for the Assessment of Children in Need and their Families (2000) – health, education, emotional and behavioural development, identity, family and social relationships, social presentation and self-care skills. Nevertheless these need to be looked at reciprocally because if one or two factors are missing it impacts upon the rest of them (DoH, 2000). The ecological model is holistic in that it focuses on the ways in which the child's developmental needs, the capability of their parents to respond appropriately to those needs and wider environmental factors interact with one another over time.

Reports for external audiences are informed by the Youth Justice Board's asset assessment tool. While the dimensions of the asset are consistent with the Framework for the Assessment of Children in Need (DoH, 2000), the fundamental difference is that it focuses on areas of a young person's life most likely to be associated with offending behaviour. This method of assessment stems from the shift in thinking about youth crime in the mid-1990s, which saw the emergence of what has become known as the risk and protective preventative paradigm or developmental prevention for children at risk (Farrington, 2000). This change reoriented assessment, bringing in the importance of the social environment (an ecological, multilevel perspective) into explanations that previously focused on psychogenic explanations of offending. Asset requires the consideration of a wide range of factors including both clinical and actuarial data. Furthermore, a pre-sentence report offers a broad opportunity to place the offending behaviour in a personal, cultural and structural context (Thompson, 1997). The ecological approach to assessment is based on the principle that the development and behaviour of individuals can be fully understood only in the context of the environments in which they live (Gill and Jack, 2007). An underlying premise of the ecological approach is that the most effective interventions occur on a compound level, taking into consideration a broad range of factors. Indeed, a number of studies have demonstrated that a range of factors at individual, community and family levels are implicated in youth crime. Individual factors include pro-criminal peers, school exclusion and substance misuse. Community factors such as economic disadvantage and lack of social cohesion are also implicated (Utting et al., 1993; Home Office, 1995; Audit Commission, 1996; Sampson et al., 1997; Rutter et al., 1998). Family factors include parental domestic violence, parental criminality, inadequate supervision, inconsistent discipline, and poor parent–child attachments. Jack and Jack (2000) propose that any attempt to prevent or reduce offending will need to address all of these factors and the interactions between them. However, cultural norms and values may have significant differences, which can result in serious misunderstandings, and this in turn can impact on the quality of the assessment (HMIP, 2000). While liaison with Ehsan's foster carers, teachers and access to available records prepared the ground for an integrated and multidisciplinary assessment, the information provided tended to be Eurocentric and it seemed that little attention had been paid to the exceptional circumstances he had experienced in his homeland and during his subsequent migration to this country. I contacted the co-ordinator (herself a refugee) of the local self-help group, Refugee First, who provided an outline of the legal position regarding applications for political asylum and she signposted me to other relevant organisations. She also gave me a valuable insight into the experiences of other asylum seekers in the city.

REFLECTION POINT

- *Think of as many reasons as you can why unaccompanied refugee/asylum-seeking children leave their home country.*

- *Where might they come from?*

- *Why might they choose to come to the United Kingdom?*

An interpreter had been engaged for the preparation of the pre-sentence report and by chance he came from a town some 50 miles away from Ehsan's hometown. Discussion with the interpreter therefore informed cultural sensitivity and increased understanding of Ehsan's circumstances. As Thakker et al., (2008) point out, a good therapeutic relationship needs to be based on respect for, and knowledge of, the client's culturally embedded customs and beliefs. A relatively recent phenomenon, the issue of unaccompanied asylum-seeking children seems to have taken social work by surprise – despite developing research there still appears to be a lack of knowledge concerning legal and political issues relating to these young people. Unlike most of the young people I work with, Ehsan had been threatened by chronic civil unrest rather than emotional or material deprivation. He had met with, and still faces, great uncertainties in relation to his past, having suddenly been uprooted from his family and home, and the prospect for the future as an asylum applicant is unsure. He was now obliged to survive in a different environment with unfamiliar rules, language and customs. Indeed, he had spent his early adolescence living in a war zone in which carrying a weapon for one's own protection is seen as a practical measure rather than a criminal offence. Documentation provided by the Crown Prosecution Service included a statement from an independent witness, who suggested that Ehsan had been the victim of a racially aggravated assault and that he committed the offence in self-defence. Indeed, Ehsan expressed that he felt a sense of injustice, explaining that he had been the victim of a serious assault by a group of men, one of whom had smashed a bottle over his head. He had retaliated by slashing one of his assailant's arms with a knife. His alleged attacker had been tried for the offence although the case was not proved and he was acquitted. However, while Ehsan was conscious that he was also a victim, his limited experience and lack of English at the time of the incident may have meant that he was not fully aware of any underlying racism that led up to the incident.

The quality and character of the child's closest relationships is considered to be the primary concept linking the set of factors that have a bearing on human development. Relationships provide the fundamental experience which link the child's personal and social world and it is within the interaction between these two worlds that the psyche forms, personality develops, behaviour evolves and social competency begins (Prior and Glaser, 2006). The primary role of the parent is to facilitate their child's develop-ment within a safe environment while balancing the child's need for socialisation and exploratory learning with the need for protection and boundary setting. The style in which the parent approaches this will be predisposed by the model of care that they themselves experienced as a child and whether they continue to be disturbed by unease around self-esteem, identity and self-control (Howe et al., 1999). Ecological approaches to assessment are based on the principle that development and behaviour of individuals can only be understood in the context of the environments in which they live (Jack, 2001). However, to look exclusively at Ehsan's needs within the context of his current circumstances would only provide part of the picture in that it would not take into account his experiences prior to coming to the UK. Separation and loss were a fundamental part of Ehsan's story but while he was willing to engage in the present, he was very reticent about revealing information about his life in Afghani-stan, would not discuss his feelings about his missing family and rejected any attempt to engage him in life-story work. Simmonds (in Kohli and Mitchell, 2002) suggests that people seeking asylum frequently regard all authority figures as a threat and feel that disclosure about their past could ultimately result in deportation. I considered the costs and benefits of Ehsan's silence. For him silence meant relative security while disclosure might bring the risk of deportation. However, his reticence could have also been a burden. Having been sent away by his family, albeit to a place of safety, he may have felt rejected. Furthermore, his family remained in Afghanistan and as Yule's (1998) research showed, young people who have escaped a war zone often carry a sense of survivor's guilt, being disorientated by their own good fortune in comparison to those who were left behind. Almost certainly the most significant people in Ehsan's life now were his foster carers, with whom he had built a close and trusting relation-ship. At the time of the initial assessment it was unclear whether Ehsan would be able to remain in their care after sentencing as this was a specialist remand placement.

Community relationships that provide social support have consistently shown to be a positive influence upon developmental outcomes for children and young people (Jack, 2001). Any migrant, whether child or adult, faces the dilemma of balancing integration into the host society with 'disintegration' from the society left behind (Bierens, et al., 2007). Research has established that the social networks of refugees and asylum seekers play an important part in the process of integration by providing both practical and emotional support. Ehsan had formed links with a local refugee group shortly after his arrival in the UK and had since made several friends among the Kurdish community in the city. These associations offer the opportunity for young people and adults to meet and share traditional food, swap stories and give and receive informal support. Another important part of social integration for young asylum seekers is education. Clements (2006) points out that while preserving their cultural and religious differences is imperative, it is nonetheless essential that unaccompanied asylum seekers are able to speak English in order to integrate into the local community. Formal education was initially a struggle for Ehsan. Although he acknowledged the importance of being able to speak English, most of the academic work assumed that the child would have literacy skills in their first language, which he lacked. With hindsight, it might have benefited Ehsan to have undertaken a more practical route, in addition to English and literacy classes, in order to build on the skills he had already learned in Afghanistan. This would have helped him to develop confidence and skills useful to him in the UK and would also be applicable, should he return to Afghanistan in the future. Nevertheless, he had a positive attitude to the social aspect of school and took full advantage of the extracurricular activities. The school environment also gave Ehsan a sense of efficacy as his teachers had indicated that he was regarded as a valued member of the Prince's Trust group at his school. He was described as a positive role model who assisted with the younger children in the group, acting as a mentor and supporter.

ACTIVITY 2.2

- *Think about the community resources that are available in your area to support unaccompanied asylum-seeking children and young people.*
- *How would you go about identifying these?*

As part of the assessment I had to balance Ehsan's needs and the potential risk to the public. The management of risk has become a progressively important concept in criminal justice social work over recent years. Risk-led practice is perceived as one of the key foundations for effective work to reduce offending among young people. For the purposes of the asset risk assessment, the term 'risk' is taken to mean: the *probability that an event or behaviour carrying the possibility of an adverse or negative outcome will occur* (Kemshall, 2001). The risk assessment aims to identify three possible outcomes: the risk of reoffending; the risk of serious harm to others; and vulnerability – that is, the risk of harm to that young person either through their own behaviour or because of the actions or omissions of others. In view of the protective factors such as a positive attitude towards education, supportive (surrogate) parents, constructive leisure activities and beneficial community links, I assessed the risk of reoffending and serious harm to others as low. Nevertheless, the seriousness of his offence meant that there was a strong possibility of a custodial sentence. Given his political status coupled with his limited English, I assessed that the prospect of custody presented serious issues of vulnerability and I made this explicit in my report. My personal belief is that the use of custody should be reserved solely for those who pose a threat to public protection. Stone (1997) suggests that a particular social work strength in advising courts is to make more evident the potentially damaging impact of imprisonment both for the offender and others in his/her life, and to challenge the value of segregation in shaping the offender's future behaviour. Therefore, my recommendation for sentence was that of a 12-month Supervision Order. The judge agreed with my risk of vulnerability assessment, remarking that he believed a custodial sentence would be harmful to Ehsan and therefore he sentenced him to a two-year Supervision Order, a requirement of which was to address Ehsan's offending behaviour.

Most theories and models of behaviour change emphasise an individual behaviour change process, yet pay little attention to socio-cultural and physical environmental influences. In order to work effectively with Ehsan I needed to find a balance between his universal and specific needs. Ehsan was by now fully aware that carrying a knife is illegal in the UK and he had indicated that he was determined not to reoffend. Therefore much of my work has been aimed at supporting him on both emotional and practical levels. While his links within the ethnic community were very important to him, most of his friends were adults and after leaving school he missed the companionship of other young people. I was aware of a multi-ethnic performing arts/dance group, which had been set up by another young person, Joe, who was a Kosovan refugee. Ehsan was hesitant at first but he agreed to meet with Joe and eventually joined the group, where he found new friends, some of whom had shared similar experiences. As our relationship developed, trust gradually increased and Ehsan felt able to impart a steady trickle of information about his family and life in Afghanistan. He was able to speak of his anguish over his missing family and he indicated that he feared his father was dead. The Red Cross had been engaged to try to locate family members in Afghanistan in accordance with the requirement of Article 221 of the United Nations Convention on the Rights of the Child (1989) but although their efforts are ongoing, no trace of the family has been found. Since coming to power in 1997 the Labour government has identified 'social exclusion' – a euphemism for disadvantage/poverty – as a major policy priority. As Bierens et al. (2007) point out, young asylum seekers are often identified as a key group at risk of social exclusion. This has been apparent when Ehsan has attempted to do practical things that most others take for granted. For example, when he went with his foster carers to open a bank account he was refused by several high-street banks on the grounds of his lack of citizenship. This was eventually resolved after several letters, phone calls and much negotiation with the sympathetic bank manager who worked at my own branch. Similarly, I later found myself liaising with the DVLA in an attempt to find a way around the bureaucratic barriers of obtaining a provisional driving licence for Ehsan. After much correspondence Ehsan eventually got his licence. Indeed, I have increasingly found myself challenging the divisive and exclusionary practices that distinguish people in Ehsan's position.

Ehsan had remained with his foster carers after sentencing but it was unclear how long after his sixteenth birthday he would be able to remain in this placement. There is evidence that age on leaving care is linked to life skills outcomes and that 17- and 18-year-old care-leavers are shown to have better outcomes than those who leave care at 16 (Biehal et al., 1995). The Children (Leaving Care) Act 2000 was introduced in order to improve services by giving young people a legal entitlement to better support in the transition to adulthood. In particular, the Act seeks to ensure that young people do not move to independent living until they are ready, and that they receive effective support once they leave care. Despite this legislative framework there is evidence that an overwhelming number of British care leavers are expected to live independently at a considerably lower age than most young people who are not looked-after children (Morgan and Lindsay, 2006). Evaluations of best practice suggest that the leaving-care transition should involve and empower the young person. Secondly, all those with an interest in the support of the young person should be fully involved in the process, if this is consistent with the young person's wishes (Biehal et al., 1995; Stein and Wade, 2000). The regulations require that the young person's wishes and feelings are taken into account (Department of Health, 2001). While his carers, his social worker and I were in agreement that it was in Ehsan's best interests to remain there until his eighteenth birthday, and Ehsan himself had indicated that he wanted to remain in the placement, it emerged that he would be expected to move on to independent living when he left school.

A report published by the NSPCC draws attention to the practice of placing unac-companied asylum-seeking young people in independent accommodation as soon as they are 16 (Tilley, 2008). As Tilley points out, this provision is inadequate for young people who have often experienced abuse and trauma and who do not have sufficient skills to cope with living independently. She suggests that the disapproving tone of public discourse about asylum contributes to an environment in which negative public attitudes to it exist, even among service providers. Tilley claims that social care pro-viders have responded by treating refugees and asylum seekers as part of the larger generic 'black and minority ethnic' category without appropriate regard for their distinct experiences and needs. Indeed, I have worked with many British care leavers, very few of whom have been able to manage adequately with the transition to independent living at the age of 16. Ehsan's limited language skills and lack of 'street wisdom' would place him at an even greater disadvantage if the transition was initiated before he was ready. Nevertheless, the manner in which he was removed from his foster carers was little short of abusive. Within weeks of him leaving school, he and his carers were given just 24 hours' notice of the plan to move him into a training flat in order to vacate the foster placement for another young person. He moved out the next day with no time to prepare for the transition and he and his carers were understandably extremely distressed. Furthermore, little attention had been given to the suitability of the accommodation provided. The 'training flat' was a bedsit in a multi-occupancy property with shared front-door access and also housed a variety of adults, some of whom were openly racist towards him and he also received threats of violence. Racists frequently seek to legitimise their attitudes by referring selectively to media reports, which imply an exaggerated link between asylum seekers and the threat of terrorism. Therefore Ehsan's experience of racism has been exacerbated by his political status. Indeed, Rutter (2007) accuses the government of increasing public resentment towards asylum seekers by their use of pejorative language. She suggests that this simply constructs a social problem in the minds of the public and triggers negative media coverage, which leads to public hostility. Understandably, Ehsan indicated that he did not feel safe there and as a result he rarely stayed in the property, preferring to 'sofa-surf' with friends from the Kurdish community. Eventually alternative, more appropriate accommodation was identified, a self-contained flat within walking distance of the home of his former foster carers' from whom he still derived considerable emotional and practical support.

While the vulnerability of unaccompanied asylum seekers is well documented, little attention has been given to the resilience that such young people often display. Indeed, many of these young people possess a capacity to respond positively to the stresses around them, bearing out that becoming a refugee is a resolute act of strength and capability. Furthermore, when compared with British looked-after children, it has been found that while a minority need psychological intervention, the vast majority are not as psychologically damaged as their British counterparts who have been harmed by their own families (Kohli and Mather, 2003). Ehsan's transition into independence, while it was not without incident, was smoothed along by his own capacity to adapt to his situation despite the pressures around him. Ehsan's political status meant that he was denied a work permit. However, he confided that he supplemented his care-leaver's allowance by repairing cars for friends and associates in the Kurdish community. He then revealed that his father had been a mechanic, running his own garage and that he had been working with him since he was a boy and had been able to drive a car since he was approximately 10 years old. Had he disclosed this information previously it would have certainly have influenced his education provision, enabling him to engage on a vocational course. However, given his ability and level of experience, he may have already known more than the instructors could teach him. As Humphries (2004) observes, many asylum seekers have the skills and motivation to make a positive contribution to society yet they are excluded from employment. She discusses governmental policing of immigration and goes on to suggest that social work has increasingly been drawn into the surveillance process. Ehsan's increasing work commitments (by now he was also working in a restaurant during the evenings) posed an ethical dilemma. While I admired his enterprise and could see that his work increased his sense of self-efficacy, I was unsure how the information that he was working illegally sat with my duty to the local authority. Following discussion during supervision I decided to do nothing with the information. While Ehsan has indicated that his long-term plan is to remain in the UK, his uncertain status adds a further dimension to assessment and planning in that consideration must be given to the fact that he might not be permitted to remain indefinitely. This uncertainty regarding his long-term future has certainly had an impact upon Ehsan and he is aware that at some point his forced return to Afghanistan may become a reality. His increasing self-sufficiency along with the skills he was developing through his employment would be of advantage should he have to return to Afghanistan in the future.

As mentioned previously, the ecological model focuses on the ways in which children's developmental needs, the capacity of their parents to respond appropriately to those needs, and the wider environmental factors interact with one another over time (Jack, 2001). The obvious gap in this assessment is the significant lack of information about Ehsan's past experiences and the capacity of his parents. However, it is worth noting that while children's experiences are germane to their development, other individual factors such as temperament, personality and gender all influence the manner in which they react to the experiences of their families and the environments in which they grow up (DoH, 2000, p5). My work with Ehsan has now ended. He completed his Supervision Order successfully and did not reoffend. He is approaching his eighteenth birthday after which a decision will be made on whether he is to be granted refugee status. If this is denied he will be deported if the Home Office deems it safe to do so. While it is my belief that young people in Ehsan's position should be regarded as a potential asset rather than just that of a responsibility under international law, with hindsight I feel that I should have done more work around preparing him for the possibility of deportation. He will have spent a significant part of his life in the UK, has lost all contact with his family and will need to make a huge social adjustment if he returns home.

This case study has described an ecological model of assessment and has highlighted some of its limitations. The quality of such an assessment is in many ways dependent on the amount and availability of information and in the case of young people such as Ehsan there are often missing pieces. Using Bronfenbrenner's model, we as social workers are ourselves a part of the child's ecosystem and the quality of social work intervention impacts on the outcomes for the individual. My work with Ehsan has highlighted a training need, not just for myself but also for my colleagues, who are beginning to pick up cases involving unaccompanied asylum seekers. In the broader context there is a need for these young people to be seen as a more legitimate social work client group. As Humphries (2004) points out, social work is a profession that deals with the most vulnerable and disadvantaged people in society and it is now challenged with some of the most subjugated people on the planet as its clients. Collet (2004) argues that social workers are inadequately trained in immigration issues. He goes on to express that while social work is an anti-discriminatory practice, immigration is an area where discrimination is allowed because of the illegitimacy ascribed to the client group. Anti-oppressive practice is one of the 'sacred cows' of social work (Wilson and Beresford, 2000, p553). However, there is a contradiction between this and our role as agents of the state with regard to immigration issues. The ethical implications of this cannot go unchallenged by the profession and, as Collet (2004) advocates, should be offered as a critique in social work training.

REFLECTION POINT

- *How well prepared are you for working with unaccompanied asylum-seeking children?*
- *Where would you go for advice?*
- *What are your own training needs in respect of working with this vulnerable group?*
- *What steps might you take to meet these needs?*

Student reflection

One of the joys of doing the Post-Qualifying Specialist Child Care Award was simply having time to pause for breath, time to read and time to reflect. *There's a whole world out there*, remarked a colleague and fellow student, looking around in some surprise. This view was particularly relevant in relation to the teaching and research around ecological factors. In the day-to-day rush of work, particularly after many years of direct work with children and families, it is very easy to lose sight of the wider picture. Undertaking this study reminded me of the overwhelming significance of the environment and social justice.

I conclude that as social workers we may see community work as beyond our skills and remit, yet nothing we could do at an individual or family level, no amount of home visiting, could improve the lives of our clients so profoundly as the changes brought about by successful community projects, building social capital and a reduction in overall levels of social inequality.

In terms of direct practice this study has highlighted the importance of social networks and social support. My practice has changed insofar as I increasingly make use of family group conferences and, in particular, look ahead for youngsters leaving care to assess and develop their support networks.

On a wider social front, discovering the work of Richard Wilkinson, volumes of meta-research on the effects of inequality, was to rediscover my revolutionary roots – a shout-it-out-loud 'yes!' moment. At last, convincing scientific evidence for the benefits of social justice!

In his work *The Impact of Inequality: How to Make Sick Societies Healthier*, Wilkinson highlights that on any measure of human well-being – health, longevity, crime, domestic violence, mental health etc. – what appears to be the most significant factor, beyond basic survival needs, is not the overall wealth of society but the wealth gap between rich and poor. In short, we will live longer and happier lives in a fairer society (Wilkinson, 2005).

This has implications for the values underlying our attitude and approach to direct practice with individuals and families and also, it seems to me, implications for our

→

ethics and politics. There is a tension in social work of which I had always been aware but of which I had rather lost sight until now. The danger is that as social workers we become part of the problem, rather than part of the solution: papering over the cracks, prolonging injustice and increasing overall suffering, if we do not also argue, loudly and clearly, the case for social justice.

FURTHER READING

For an update on the current situation in relation to services for disabled children and their families read:

DfES. Department for Education and Skills (2007) *Aiming high for disabled children: Better support for families.* HM Treasury.
Available at: **www.hm-treasury.gov.uk/d/cyp_disabled_children18057.pdf** (Accessed 15 April 2009).

Border and Immigration Agency (2008) *Better outcomes: The way forward – Improving the care of unaccompanied asylum-seeking children.* The Home Office. Available at:
www.bia.homeoffice.gov.uk/sitecontent/documents/aboutus/consultations/closedconsultations/uasc/betteroutcomes.pdf?view=Binary (Accessed 17 April 2009).

Chapter 3

Legislation and social policy

Contributors: Mike Coleman, Hilary Schultess-Young and Steven Mills

ACHIEVING A POST-QUALIFYING SPECIALIST AWARD IN CHILD CARE

The practical application of legislation and social policy is fundamental to a social worker's understanding and carrying out of their professional role. The continual changes to national legislation and social policy often provide a challenge for managers to afford their social work staff time to take on the changes and consider how it underpins their work.

By introducing the legislation and social policy unit we wanted to provide the students with an opportunity to explore key relevant legislation and enable them to demonstrate a critical understanding of its application with reference to individual casework examples.

The primary aim of the unit was to impart to the students knowledge of the law and emphasise the empowering effect it can have in their everyday practice as social workers, if understood and applied correctly. This chapter will help you to develop the required knowledge base for legislation and social policy.

- Key legislation, regulation and guidance.
- Application of legislation and guidance to practice.
- The impact of local agency policy and procedures.
- Social policy initiatives in relation to child care practice.
- Roles and responsibilities of other key professionals.

A lecturer's perspective on the delivery of legislation and policy
The teaching of legislation and policy is often regarded by many professionals as dry and uninteresting. The fact that social workers have the opportunity to consult with legal services within their local authority, should casework require it, can leave the social worker in believing that the task of identifying how casework should proceed was simply down to another profession. The majority of students at the beginning of the legislation/policy unit felt that casework was often directed by the decisions made by legal services and they had a 'duty' to respond to the decisions made. In some cases these decisions left the social worker feeling uneasy about how the case was proceeding, but they ultimately had little choice.

$\rightarrow$

I felt the task of delivering a series of law lectures to experienced child care practitioners, from a variety of child care settings, would be a challenge, particularly meeting the programme's aims together with the expectation of the students. It was essential that I covered some key legislation, e.g. Children Act 1989/2004, to ensure that all students had a fundamental understanding of the most relevant legislation. However, it was also essential to challenge the students in both their knowledge of the law and how to use it as a tool within their everyday practice.

One of the key pieces of legislation was the Human Rights Act 1989. Although the majority of students were aware of this legislation, very few had a practical grasp of it as a piece of legislation that had significant implications for their working practice. Exploring the Human Rights Act 1989 with the student group gave them time to consider how 'everyday' decisions taken in practice had to be considered in light of this law. The Human Rights Act could no longer just be accorded 'lip service', but had to become real and relevant to the practitioner. The students responded favourably to this input and were able to give casework examples where they had failed to take into consideration the implications of human rights in respect of the child and respective carers. The implications for these decisions would not only have been potentially detrimental to the child/carers but also for the social worker and their respective employing body should they have been challenged in a court of law.

In addition this led to a detailed examination of the law relating to judicial review, and how important it was for them to appreciate that all decisions made by a social worker can be subject to judicial review which imposed upon them the importance of ensuring detailed case notes, which demonstrated a reasoned decision-making process, which in turn emphasised that this was the foundation stone of good professional practice.

Another objective within the delivery of the legislation unit was affording the students the time to explore both national and local policy in context to their employing agency. Many students within their written assignment took the opportunity to explore how their legislative role had evolved and how policy decisions, made at both national and local level, inform their everyday practice. The students enjoyed the opportunity to discuss how varying agencies had interpreted legislation differently and local policy evolved to meet agency resources rather than local need. The students began to see that key legislation, interpreted differently, often resulted in them working in a very different environment than their neighbouring authorities.

One other key task within the unit was exploring the role of the 'expert witness'. It became evident that some social workers considered their professional role to be lesser than that of an 'expert witness' and I emphasised that 'expert' evidence is merely opinion evidence and therefore as professional social workers they were able to question, and if need be, challenge the conclusions of the 'expert witness'. I was trying to stress that as professionals themselves they were not only entitled to challenge these conclusions if they raised grave concern or doubt in their own

→

minds but were under a duty to do so. This specific role often appeared to be viewed by the student as necessary to convince a court that the decision their agency was making on a case gave it some validity. The students often did not consider, or believe, that they themselves often had more expertise in what they were presenting, than inviting the 'expert witness' to the court setting. Inviting the students to look at presenting evidence in a court setting allowed the student to begin to see the importance of casework recording, preparation of evidence, and presenting themselves in court appeared to give them confidence.

Professional accountability, introduced in this unit, also gave the students a basis to consider their professional practice. Reviewing the GSCC's Code of Practice provided the basis of them understanding the legal implications of their professional role. As social care professionals social workers are subject to the stringent requirements of professional responsibility, the essence of which is accountability. Emphasis was placed upon the many ways in which social workers are accountable for the standard of their professional practice which is particularly relevant post-Climbié. In addition to examining the social workers' professional standards, the GSCC's Code of Practice for Managers was also examined and how the interplay between the dynamic of the two roles can affect quality of the service provided, which is also subject to the same professional scrutiny.

The legislation unit allowed the students to identify that legislation is not imposed on them, but provides them with a working tool to consider everyday decisions being made by them in practice. Numerous students identified that they had always considered that they could not 'use' legislation/policy to aid them in their practice and optimal outcomes for service users, but had considered it a straitjacket to the decision-making process. The students' competence to undertake complex legislative work was rarely in question; the issue appeared to be around the students' confidence in undertaking this work and I believe the law unit aided the students in their transition.

Child care law and policy – a human rights perspective

Developments in social policy and legislation appear to be shaped by the reaction to tragic child deaths and the perceived malpractice of social workers. This has meant that there has been a reactive rather than proactive approach to social policy and legislation. The resulting investigations have focused on the conduct of the professionals involved rather than analysing the ideals and norms of society that are precipitated and prejudiced by such circumstances (Fawcett et al., 2004). The political ethos of the time also dictates the direction and implementation of policy and legislation (Denney, 1998).

Children's services in my local authority are currently subject to the government's plan to reorganise such services which affects my practice as a social worker for the local authority (Fawcett et al., 2004). Using some examples from my practice, I will demonstrate the impact of child care legislation, national policies and how they are interpreted at a local level. Before analysing particular cases, it is necessary to understand the historical context to child care in the United Kingdom.

Why the Children Act 1989?

Prior to the implementation of the Children Act 1989, the Conservative government was alarmed to discover the extent of child abuse within children's homes perpetrated by those entrusted to care for the most vulnerable children in society. The Welsh Office in particular was found to have been lacking in its vigilance and procedures for investigating allegation of abuse, and systematic abuse was widespread (Daniel and Ivatts, 1998). The 1988 Cleveland Inquiry also had an impact on the passage of the Children Act through Parliament and arguably contributed to the Act's emphasis on the responsibilities of parents (Corby, 2000).

Introducing the legislation

The Children Act 1989 is a landmark piece of legislation that attempts to create a whole code of law about the upbringing of children. It aims to bring about the best for children, within the bounds of legislation, whether they are living within families, in need of local authority services or in need of protection from abuse. The guiding principle of the Act is that of working in partnership with parents. The Act emphasises the importance of parental responsibility and lays a duty on local authorities to support parents, including their involvement as much as possible when children are looked after by the state, even when they are the subject of a care order.

A greater role for the courts was seen as a way of strengthening the position of parents dealing with social work agencies. The Act has also attempted to strengthen the rights of children to be involved in decisions that affect them and to place greater emphasis on the extended family (Brayne and Martin, 1999). The notable feature of part III of the Act is the recurring reference to the term *children in need*. The definition is precise and refers to the local authority providing services to children who could not achieve or maintain a reasonable standard of health or development without assistance or if the child is disabled. The Act's intention is to ensure that the most vulnerable children receive appropriate services and are protected and reviewed in partnership with parents (Allen, 2001).

The Warner Report, *Choosing With Care* (DoH and Welsh Office, 1992) identified complacency in the protection of looked-after children and for the need for robust systems for the vetting of all current and prospective residential care workers. In 1995 the Department of Health produced a code of practice for the employment of residential care workers which followed clear recommendations from the Warner Report.

The Utting Report, *People Like Us* (DoH and Welsh Office, 1997) went much further and proposed a protective strategy to safeguard the children living away from home and recognised the need for stringent measures for protecting against and exposing abuse. The need to raise the national standards of registration and inspection within all forms of child care provision was identified to ensure that any gaps could not be exploited by dubious providers or potential abusers. The Protection of Children Act 1999 was passed to prevent any paedophiles from working with children.

The political agenda – New Labour

The Labour Party came into power in 1997 and accepted all of Sir William Utting's recommendations and incorporated these in the DoH's Quality Protects initiative (1998). It is important to recognise the government's own political agenda at this time. In May 1998 a national child care strategy was launched to tackle the issue of social exclusion. It had been identified that in 1997 there were 4.4 million children living in households who, using the government's own official measure, were living in poverty. The government set about ending child poverty by increasing child benefit and introducing a new Working Family Tax Credit and Child Tax Credit. This achieved the lifting of half a million children out of poverty, but still left the poorest 20 per cent of households with only 6 per cent of the national income, compared with 45 per cent in the top fifth. Interestingly, twice as many disabled children live in the poorest households as in the richest (Dobson and Middleton, 1999).

The modernisation agenda

The *Modernising of Social Services* White Paper was published in 1998, acknowledged the need for improvements and highlighted the need to raise standards in the care and protection of children living away from home. It introduced eight regional, independent, inspection watchdogs, (Commissions for Care Standards) to impose strict standards for all care homes and other care resources. Also, new methods for checking that councils were delivering efficient and quality services were also introduced, i.e. performance indicators and best value Initiative.

The government saw the Quality Protects programme as the cornerstone of its modernisation agenda for children and family services. They laid out very clear objectives for all social services departments. There were originally eight objectives that encompassed the findings of the Utting Report, with three further objectives included later. The objectives equally applied to children with disabilities and it recognised that effective partnerships with education, health and the voluntary sector are essential. One of the objectives specifically applies to children with disabilities living within the community and states that their needs must be assessed and reviewed. All 11 objectives lay out very clear expectations, with National Priorities Guidance Targets being set. This has produced an element of competition between councils as statistical comparisons and league tables become the accepted norm. The winners enjoyed three-star status, less scrutiny and more money; the losers were placed on special measures, greater levels of inspection and their community was penalised with less funding (Daniel and Ivatts, 1998).

It could be argued that this was an introduction of a somewhat prescriptive and draconian regime. However, children in the care of the local authorities had been let down and a succession of governments had failed to meet their moral obligations to the most vulnerable members of society as well as the under-funding of the welfare system. These and other government initiatives have been designed to address levels of serious inequality and disadvantage for many children in the UK. However, there is bound to be a question mark over the longer-term viability of this investment if the country's economic prosperity is not maintained (Jones, 2001).

The government has admitted that the Sure Start scheme for under fives and policies for children in care have failed the socially excluded. The Prime Minister talking on 15 May 2006 stated that Sure Start has failed to reach families that are 'out of the system'. He admitted that there is a lack of cohesion among agencies working in these areas. The Prime Minister said at the time:

> If we are frank about it, there is a group of people who have been shut out against society's mainstream and we have not yet found a way of bringing them properly in. When we started Sure Start – there was an idea that it would lift all the boats on a rising tide. It has not worked like that. Sure Start has been brilliant for those people who have, in their own minds, decided they want to participate. But the hard to reach families, the ones who are shut out of the system . . . they are not going to come to places like Sure Start.

> (*The Guardian*, 16 May, 2006)

The DoH Framework for the Assessment of Children and their Families (2000) was devised to enable local authorities to implement the Quality Protects programme. Quality Protects remains central to the government's attempt to transform the management and delivery of services to children. The Framework aims to improve the life chances of the most vulnerable and disadvantaged children by providing a systematic method of assessment and recording, thus enabling informed judgements to be made about whether the child is in need, or is suffering, or likely to suffer significant harm. The Children Act Report (2000) highlighted that 55 per cent of households with children with a disability are living in poverty and 11 per cent of children receiving help from social services are disabled. A quarter of children looked after have a disability, compared with less than 4 per cent of the general population. This is a very high over-representation.

Moving towards a preventative approach

It was envisaged that the Framework would counterbalance the past practice of children's services departments to target a majority of their time and resources on child protection at the expense of children in need (DoH, 1995). The Framework requires the social worker to explore the wider ecological picture rather than focusing on the narrow confines of the nuclear family (Jack and Owen, 2003). This emphasis on taking a preventative approach to social work rather than reactive child protection strategies has been endorsed by the current Every Child Matters protocol and the introduction of the Children Act 2004 (Jackson, 2005). Local authorities are required to lead on integrated service delivery through multi-agency trusts. In my local authority this meant that social services and the local education authority merged in 2005/6 into Services for Children, Young People and Families.

As part of this reform, social workers responsible for children with disabilities have now moved from the community care team to become part of children services. However, the changeover is far from smooth as the children with disabilities team currently has a high referral rate, is short of resources and at present short of managers and direction. This is particularly concerning as children with disabilities are at increased vulnerability of all forms of abuse due to greater dependency on carers for intimate care, communication difficulties and less stringent safeguards (DoH, 1999).

Article 12 of the Convention on the Rights of the Child (1991) instructs all signed-up nations to fully integrate disabled children into the community. It states an obligation that requires the children's views and feelings to be heard. This was the first international document to stress the child's rights to autonomy, respect, participation and voice (Freeman, 1995). In reality, children with disabilities are often lost in the care system, hidden away in long-stay institutions and hospitals, with children's services having little knowledge of their personal circumstances, let alone knowing how they feel (Morris, 1998).

Rights and responsibilities

The Human Rights Act 1998 came into force on 2 October 2000. The Act is one of the most important pieces of constitutional legislation enacted in the United Kingdom.

Arising out of the horrors of the Second World War, the European Convention on Human Rights established a universal system of human rights and the UK government became a signatory to the Convention on 3 September 1953. The Human Rights Act 1998 incorporates the Convention rights into UK legislation and is binding on the UK government in international law. Courts at all levels are required to abide by the Act. The most significant article of the Human Rights Act with regard to my practice as a social worker, is Article 8, which states that everyone has a right to respect for his private and family life, his home and his correspondence (Brayne and Carr, 2005).

The Act makes it a statutory responsibility that, particularly with regard to safeguarding and care proceedings, any interference must be balanced, justified, in the best interests of the child with a transparent and accountable decision-making process (Brayne and Carr, 2005).

ACTIVITY 3.1

- *The law guides our practice, but can it tell us everything? What guidelines do you have in your agency to enable sound professional practice?*
- *What is the status of these guidelines and how do they impact on your practice?*
- *How does your agency work with service users to inform policy in your practice?*

Examples from practice

Daisy was born with a heart defect which required immediate surgery. Her recovery was slow after the operation and she remained on a ventilator for a considerable period of time. Daisy required several re-admissions due to recurrent chest infections and seizures. Daisy suffered medical complications, including having to be fed by a tube. Her mother, Sharon, struggled to come to terms with her daughter's disability. Sharon is a white, single parent. Daisy was born out of a brief relationship and the father's whereabouts were not known as he effectively 'disappeared' after Sharon told him she was pregnant.

Children's services were alerted by health professionals when Sharon failed to visit the hospital and there was concern that Sharon was rejecting Daisy. There is a plethora of government initiatives, social policy and legislation that has an impact on the quality and type of service delivery for Daisy and Sharon. The Children Act 1989 emphasises that children with disabilities are children first. The Disability Discrimination Act 1995 states that social services and health must not discriminate against people with disabilities by offering a lower standard of service. The Human Rights Act 1998 requires local authorities to respect the rights of the individual under Article 14 (prohibition of discrimination) but fails to treat people with a disability as a group that needs particular consideration.

The Framework of Assessment (DoH, 2000) emphasises inclusion and quality of service as key values, but there is no reference regarding the institutional discrimination of people with disabilities. It is apparent that children who have physical, sensory and/or intellectual impairment have often been treated as inferior humans, resulting in discrimination and segregation (Morris, 1998). Stantham and Reed (1998) highlighted that the demands made on parents and carers of disabled children go well beyond what is expected of parents of non-disabled children. Sharon not only had to come to terms with Daisy's disabilities, but had to consider whether she could look after Daisy for the rest of her life, even with the assistance of support services. Definitions and language play a very important part in how individuals and organisations can understand disability. To individualise the 'problem' as Daisy's impairment and to concentrate on her functional and psychological losses would not be uncommon.

Oliver (1999) suggests that organisations should avoid looking at children with disabilities from a deficit perspective, as this is oppressive, but instead apply a social model that uses the term 'disability' to describe the prejudice and discrimination, lack of opportunities and social barriers that people with disabilities encounter everyday. But the reality for Daisy is that the local authority continues to struggle to provide parity for children with disabilities, despite the legislation.

I was involved with this case when children with disabilities were the responsibility of adult services. The logic given for this was that this service user group had chronic needs and required a 'cradle to grave' service. However, there were few specialist workers within the team. The social workers were primarily responsible for adults and did not have any specific training. The Social Services Inspectorate in 1998 reported that specialist workers are often ill-informed about child protection issues and that the welfare of children with disabilities is not always central to their practice. It is only in the last six months that I have attended child protection training with my colleagues in the Children with Individual Needs team. This has coincided with the setting up of such a team as part of the new Children, Young People and Families Service.

The protocols for joint working between our respective teams are the same as when children with disabilities were under adult social services. Lead responsibility remains with the disability team in all planning and assessment of need but the childcare team action all Child Protection and Looked-After Children procedures. This also includes addressing gaps in parenting skills. This continued split can cause information to become lost, misinterpreted or not valued as relevant by the other.

The Framework for Assessment (2000) format is not exclusively for section 47 (Children Act 1989) child protection inquiries; all section 17 (Children Act 1989) should be assessed in this way. Adult social services received no formal training in this process. The new Individual Needs Team, made up of social workers who were previously from adult social services, have still received no training and use their own generic, in-house assessment form devised eight years ago. This format is also used for adults experiencing mental health difficulties, and the elderly, as well as adults and children with disabilities. At the time of this case, unless adult social services deemed that there were child protection issues regarding children with disabilities, it was unlikely that children's services would ever know of their existence. Furthermore, it is still the case that workers who have little or no training regarding child protection issues are put in a position where they would have to refer to the childcare teams regarding safeguarding issues when they are deficient in recognising and understanding such issues. I consider this as a form of organisational discrimination that gives an implicit message that disabled children and their families do not deserve equal rights of service compared to all other children.

The first time that children's services knew of Daisy's situation was when Health and Adult Services considered Sharon was rejecting her daughter at 15 months of age and care proceedings could be required to secure her future. I was the allocated duty worker on the day of the referral and I was allocated the case. One of my first jobs was to undertake the considerable amount of checks required. These ranged from the Joint Consultancy Team to the police. I paid due regard to the Human Rights Act 1998 which came into force on 2 October 2000. Prior to this Act there was a tendency to undertake such checks without having the appropriate consent or remit. This was an abuse of power and bad practice and since the introduction of the Human Rights Act 1998 I have certainly ensured my own practice abides by the Act. While experience and research show that it is vital for professionals to share information to ensure the safety of children (reinforced by Lord Laming in 2003), it should be undertaken with consent and be proportionate. An exception to this would be if a child was at risk of immediate harm or consulting with parents would further endanger the child. This did not apply with Daisy and Sharon, so I was required under the Children Act 1989 and the Human Rights Act 1998 to obtain permission from Sharon (Brayne and Carr, 2005).

The first objective of the Quality Protects initiative states that social services need to ensure that children are securely attached to their primary carers and that effective care can be sustained for the duration of their childhood. Under section 85 of the Children Act 1989, social services also have a duty to assess the welfare of a child who has been in hospital for longer than three consecutive months. Daisy had spent most of her life in hospital and the long-term prognosis is extremely poor. The DoH (1999) *The Government's Objectives for Children's Social Services* reiterates the Children Act 1989 when it stresses the need for inter-agency working and for the 'corporate' responsibilities for children in need. The Framework stipulates that Health Authorities and Primary Care Groups and Trusts should participate in inter-agency working to promote a child's welfare and provide 'joined up services'. This has been further strengthened by section 10 of the Children Act 2004, which facilitates arrangements to promote co-operation between the local authority children services and relevant partner agencies. Although social services and education have now been merged, health remains very much separate in structure and practice.

Ruth Marchant in 1999 defined a child with complex needs as having complicated and compound requirements. It is in these circumstances that agencies need to pool their knowledge, skills and resources and also need to co-ordinate future services. Parents of disabled children have probably been subjected to many forms of assessment and many of the questions they are asked can be upsetting and only duplicate what has been asked already. The Audit Commission (1998) discovered that in only 25 per cent of circumstances did parents feel that care arrangements were well coordinated. This questions whether services lack flexibility.

Under the Quality Protects programme, local authorities are obliged to produce annual service plans, hold a central register of children with disabilities (also required under Schedule 2 of the Children Act 1989) and promote the range of services they may offer. On a positive note, they produce an excellent annual service guide that keeps service users well informed.

Banks (2001) emphasises that it is unethical and ineffective not to fully share objectives, plans and information with service users and this can be further strengthened by open recording and written agreements. At the time of this case a pilot scheme funded by the government's Health Action Zone initiative had been set up which allowed for children with complex needs to have a new service, allowing for a single assessment and planning approach between all statutory and voluntary service providers. In this case it worked well to avoid duplication of assessments and allowed a co-ordinated, balanced range of services to be provided. It also promoted full participation during assessment and subsequent reviews by Sharon.

Every Child Matters and integrated working

With the advent of the new integrated children's services and the transfer of children with disabilities to this service, the intention is to further improve this practice. The Every Child Matters protocol and the introduction of the Children Act 2004 have led to the emphasis, once again, on taking a preventative approach to social work, rather than reactive safeguarding strategies, and it became a requirement of local authorities to lead on integrated service delivery through multi-agency trusts by 2008 (Jackson, 2005). The idea of a single assessment approach is to be extended across all children's services with the intended introduction of the Common Framework of Assessment. Its purpose is to encourage the practitioners to record the first point of contact with a child and family so that it can be shared with other services, thus negating the need for repetition of assessment. Cornwall are running four individual Common Assessment Projects (CAP) pilots to test how the process can facilitate services to come together at an earlier point to address needs and prevent them from becoming more serious. However, the DfES (2005) has stated in its guidance that as children with a learning or physical disability will certainly be working with other agencies, it is unlikely that a CAP will be required. This supports the viewpoint that children with learning or physical disabilities continue to be marginalised in society (McClaughlin et al., 2005).

The ecological approach in practice

In Sharon's case, I have no doubt that the ecological model of working proved a turning point. She was able to see for herself that all the professionals involved were working towards one plan and that she was an essential contributor and component of that plan. Her confidence in the help and support Sharon received in the community enabled her to overcome her serious doubts and slowly it was observed that her attachment to Daisy improved. A transfer to an adapted bungalow close to where her own mother lives, advice on benefits made available by way of the Carers and Disabled Children's Act 2000 and the offer of respite care on Daisy's discharge from hospital made the prospect of parenting Daisy seem achievable. The joint working and re-empowerment of Daisy averted care proceedings.

If the situation had been different and Sharon was unable to care for Daisy, then there is overwhelming evidence that adoption offers the best hope of long-term stability in family life for any child who is unable to remain with their birth family (Thomas and Jackson, 1999). The Human Rights Act 1998, Children Act 1989 and the ratification of the United Nations Convention on the Rights of the Child 1991 have greatly influenced the Adoption and Children Act 2002. The present government has promoted a less restrictive attitude to the acceptance of would-be adoptive parents and removed many of the previous difficulties, e.g. by promoting open adoption and paying allowances. Consideration of permanence for Looked-After children at the four-month statutory review is now a legal obligation (Brayne and Carr, 2005). However, there is an argument that the government's agenda, with regard to adoption, is also about cost. Adoption has always been at the expense of other approaches, including more support for children to remain with their own family (Ryburn, 1998).

I also gave due regard to the Human Rights Act 1998. Article 8 states that everyone has a right to family life, but there are limits to this as it is a qualified right. Interference is permitted with regard to this right if it is in accordance with the law and necessary in a democratic society in the interests of national security, public safety, economic well-being of the country, prevention of crime or disorder, protection of health or morals or the freedoms and rights of others (Brayne and Carr, 2005). This has implications for social workers undertaking safeguarding work as justification has to be given for such interference. However, human rights can also be breached if there is inaction, such as failing to protect the interests of a vulnerable child (White et al., 2005).

The safeguarding agenda

With regard to Daisy and Sharon it was necessary for me to balance the rights (as described in Article 8) of the parent, Sharon, and Daisy's right to be protected from any neglect or abuse and to have a safe upbringing. I also had to pay due regard to the fact that although the department's intervention in family life is covered by the Children Act 1989 and allows section 47 investigations to secure the welfare of others, any action has to be proportionate and any restriction on family life has to be at the lowest level. If any action is deemed disproportionate it is a violation of Article 8 of the Human Rights Act 1998 (White et al., 2005). This had great bearing on the case, as there was considerable pressure from some quarters in the initial stages of the case, to begin care proceedings. However, it was my professional opinion that this course of action would have been against Article 8, as the planning and successful implementation of the multi-agency care plan (most importantly including Sharon) enabled me to correctly balance the rights of Sharon to enjoy family life and Daisy's rights to be protected and cared for appropriately. I believe that this course of action was compatible with Article 8 and reflected the three key operating principles of the legislation, namely: the rule of law, legitimate aims and proportionality (Brayne and Carr, 2005).

Conclusion

Legislation and social policy are always likely to develop and change. They are as much a reflection of the government's political agenda as they are the desire to improve society (Fawcett et al., 2005). The sad thing is that the current changes to children's services are not met with additional resources. On a positive note, I believe that the Human Rights Act 1998 is conducive to good practice, as Article 8 means that we have to justify our actions as they impact on family life, act in a proportionate manner and be anti-oppressive in our practice. (Brayne and Carr, 2005).

ACTIVITY 3.2

- *What is your experience of the dividing line between the right to family life (Article 8 HRA 1998) and the duty to safeguard (CA 1989)?*
- *Can you think of a current case in which the right to family life (Article 8) is overridden by the duty to safeguard?*

'No legal place to stay' – issues for Gypsy and Traveller children

Gypsies and travellers have the same basic need for a safe and secure home as anyone else in our society. However, there are two major factors that distinguish Gypsy travellers from other communities. The first is that travellers' homes are not fixed in one place or made of bricks and mortar. Instead their home may be a wagon, a caravan, a truck, a trailer or (in the old days) a tent. (Johnson and Willers, 2004). The second is that *over a third of the 600,000 travellers in the U.K. today have nowhere legal they can put their homes so live on roadsides with no amenities* (Johnson and Willers, 2004, p1). It is their plight that I will centre on in this study.

For hundreds of years Gypsy travellers have been victim to prejudicial and discriminatory legislation that has persecuted, banished and even executed them for living in the UK. The first part of my study will focus on the historical perspective of site provision, planning law, and the impact of homelessness on Gypsy traveller families.

I will examine the influence that the present human rights and race relations legislation and social policy has had on Gypsy travellers and how this has informed partnership agencies and helped Gypsy travellers in their struggle to secure a safe and protected home life. I will discuss the local scene and how national policy and guidance inform local authority practice. I will detail the local authorities' responsibility to homeless Gypsy travellers and the communities' participation in the multi-agency decision-making plans for new sites.

Throughout I will discuss my role co-ordinating Welfare Health Education Needs (WHEN) assessments with families facing eviction and my work with colleagues, carrying out our duties under current law, policy and guidance.

Definition

I define Gypsy travellers as Romany Gypsy and Irish heritage travellers, who are distinct minority ethnic groups as defined by the Race Relations Act 1976 and the Amended Act 2000. New travellers do not have minority ethnic status but qualify in planning terms as 'Gypsies' because they have a *nomadic habit of life in which their wanderings are purposeful* (Friends and Families of Travellers (FFT), 2007, p1). New travellers across the UK are unlikely to be on authorised sites, as Chapel (1993) describes: *in Cornwall there is no authorised site provision for New Travellers and unauthorised sites lack basic facilities and are on dangerous derelict grounds, polluted with toxic waste* (p3).

I will use the term 'Gypsy traveller' to describe these three communities. As the DoH (2004, p2) states: *Using the generic term Gypsy Traveller to encompass all three does not disregard group difference as each of these groups has a separate ethnic (and lifestyle) identity but they share many aspects in common.* I will, however, use specific terms when describing one community or another where necessary.

Historical and political context

The historical relationship between Romany Gypsies and the state of England dates back to 1530 with the passing of the Egyptian Act. This law was aimed at *ridding the country of all Gypsies by banning immigration and 'voluntarily' requiring them to leave within sixteen days* (Traveller Advice Team (TAT), p1). Those that didn't conform faced the removal of their possessions, imprisonment and deportation.

This law extended later to execution unless the Gypsies abandoned their *naughty, idle, ungodly life and company and adopted a sedentary way of life with a settled occupation* (Johnson and Willers, 2005, p3). Many Gypsies were executed until 1660 when state executions stopped, though punitive and restrictive laws continued.

These extremes of mistreatment have formed the basis, as Cemlyn (1995) suggests, of *the rejection of Travellers' way of life . . . and the expression of exclusion or assimilation* (p278). It seems that as the Department of Communities and Local Government (DCLG) (2004, p6) points out that *if deemed to be 'useful' those who worked on farms, were blacksmiths, entertainers etc. . . . and now casual labour are tolerated, but soon moved on when no longer so*.

Romany Gypsies and Irish heritage travellers (who migrated to England in the 1800s) survived on the edge of society until the outbreak of the Second World War, when they became a useful source of labour to help with the war effort and sites were provided.

This history has served to strengthen the importance of:

> *having a close knit community, the significant status of children for future survival, the wisdom of elders, and core to the culture travelling with extended family.*

> (Jenkins, 2006, p5)

The post-war period saw continued toleration of Gypsies and travellers as there was plenty of work to be done on reconstruction; however, this was short lived as land became scarce, which led to tighter controls about where Gypsy travellers could locate their caravans. According to Johnson and Willers (2004):

> *The scarcity of land brought about tighter immigration laws although the UK signed the Convention on Stateless Persons (1954) which states: 'the contracting states shall as far as possible facilitate the assimilation and naturalisation of stateless persons' but in practice the Home Office ignores this convention.*

> (p43)

According to Jordan (2001, p527) the Blair government overcame the legacy of the Thatcher/Major years by tackling *issues of inequality, division, and conflict by redefining social justice in terms of opportunity and community*. Gypsy traveller families who are homeless and living in poverty are not recipients of a social policy that offers community choice and opportunity. They are reliant upon the laws and policy of the land to change to enable them to escape their often abysmal circumstances.

Jordan (2001, p528) goes on to say that *social work should be an instrument for community opportunity programmes as it favours personal services and face to face transactions between officials and citizens*. The experience of many Gypsy travellers communities is that they are highly unlikely to receive assistance and support from sensitive, culturally aware welfare agencies. Their association with officials when they stop on roadsides is more likely to involve evictions, arrests and vehicle impoundments.

Stopping places for Gypsy travellers are called 'sites'. There are two types of sites: authorised, which as the FFT (2007, p1) explain: *are either privately or council run that have planning permission*, and unauthorised, where *there is no planning permission the land can be owned by Gypsy Travellers themselves, a private landowner, or public land owned by the council, the forestry commission etc....*

Current attitudes

Even today these prejudicial views are evident. A recent MORI poll found one-third of adults admitted being personally prejudiced towards Gypsies and Irish travellers; this was a higher proportion than admitted prejudice against any other group (CRE, 2003, p2). The YWCA (2006, p2) explains:

> *Young Gypsies and Travellers face racism every day, it is regular and frequent and may take the form of name calling, violent attacks, restricted access to commercial and public services, lack of accommodation or lack of political representation.*

The FFT (2007, p1) explain the lack of support from the state to provide sites limited Gypsy travellers' ability to buy small plots of land. So even those living on farms were pushed on to the roadside, as the FFT (2007, p1) continue:

> *planning does not enable, it hinders this group of people in attaining the most basic of human needs...a secure place to live, which provides basic accommodation consistent with ethnic or cultural needs.*

The issues

The 1968 Caravans Sites Act placed a duty on local authorities to provide sites to those Gypsy travellers residing and resorting to their areas. However, yet again, not enough sites were provided. Therefore any Gypsy travellers not able to find a pitch were *hounded out of the area...and those families on a pitch were afraid to leave the site knowing when they returned a pitch would probably no longer be available* (Johnson et al., 2005, p46).

This provision saw the social structure of Gypsy traveller families under threat. Unable to travel, they could not keep social networks and get employment, their culture was challenged as the rules and conditions on sites were incompatible with their traditions, i.e. no large family groups, no animals, no bonfires, etc. Cemlyn (1995) claims:

This enforced condition for many Traveller families impacts negatively on their children's health and development...this is a situation of societal imposed neglect where children bear the brunt of oppression.

(p281)

The relationship between Gypsy travellers and social work has also been problematic. Cemlyn (1995, p287) points out: *Gypsies have lost children into the care system for a variety of reasons often unconnected with their parenting skills and commitment, sometimes reflecting lack of support for their lifestyle.*

I was very aware when I first took my post that I was inheriting a past of discriminatory laws, policy and practice and for this reason I anticipated difficulties accessing the community and building relationships and trust. I felt it was important to adopt a multicultural model which, as Trevithick (2002, p48) describes, *differentiates between difference and deficiency by acknowledging the strengths and limitations that all cultural groups possess.*

However, Gypsy travellers have always been targeted for failing to live as the settled community and their situation got worse following an influx of new travellers in the 1980s. The Conservative government passed the Criminal Justice and Public Order Act 1994 Part V, which *greatly increased the powers of the police and local authorities to evict Travellers camping illegally and removed the duty on local authorities under the 1968 Act to provide sites* (FFT, 2007, p2). This repeal affected the whole community as not only were sites not built, existing ones were closed down.

New travellers faced harsh legal harassment which did not take account of their situation, as Cemlyn (1995) describes: *many had taken to the road because of acute difficulties they faced in settled society...New Travellers sites provide a supportive environment for families and vulnerable young people* (p281). I myself have found approximately 70 per cent of the new travellers I work with, as children in the care system, are estranged from their families and have other related difficulties.

The government suggested to critics of the 1994 Act that Gypsy travellers should buy their own land. However, as the FFT (2007) discusses, *the way the planning system operates means extreme marginalisation and prejudice against Travellers and official indifference to the impoverished position of this minority ethnic group* (p2). The success rate of planning applications for Gypsy travellers at appeal is *29% while for the settled community it is 89%* (Johnson et al., 2004, p47). Moreover, planning granted for Gypsy travellers is often only temporary. These appeals have placed a strain upon the community, who report they have suffered *increased marital breakdown, depression based illness, despair and gross insecurity, which all impact negatively on the children* (FFT, 2007, p3).

Assuming that one of the functions of the planning system is to ensure that people have their basic needs (e.g. accommodation) satisfied, it is clear that one-third of Gypsy travellers have been let down by the planning system to a remarkable degree.

Although nomadism and unauthorised camping are not in themselves illegal, the legislation has criminalised a way of life. In addition to this, the systematic closure of traditional stopping places through ditching, gating and boulders has resulted in Gypsy travellers having to stop on contaminated land. This has had devastating consequences, especially for pregnant women and families with young children. Jenkins (2006, p4) explains:

> *Gypsies and Travellers are often living in substandard environmental conditions where the land is polluted and unfit for habitation and poses a danger.*

She goes on to say *they are living without basic amenities of toilets, water, sewage facilities and waste collection* (2006, p5).

Further challenges

The Department of the Environment, Transport and the Regions launched a *Good Practice Guide on Managing Unauthorised Camping* in 1998 and in 2004 the Office of the Deputy Prime Minister (ODPM – aka Department of Communities and Local Government) and the Home Office launched the *Guidance on Managing Unauthorised Encampments*. The guidance states that local authorities and the police need to take into account fully the circumstances of Gypsy travellers before evicting. The DoH (2004, p2) emphasises:

> *Gypsies and Travellers are socially excluded ethnic groups, which, on the basis of existing small scale and anecdotal evidence, have specific health (welfare and education) needs that have not been systematically assessed.*

It is this guidance from the ODPM (2004) and the research by the DoH (2004) that has informed all my work with Gypsy travellers and more specifically my practice when co-ordinating WHEN assessments. Social work, according to Trevithick (2002), is *'Euro-centric', based on middle-class values, and made up mostly of white middle-class people* (p48). To avoid having this narrow vision it is important in my work that the community defines themselves, their lives and their values, which enables me to really understand the physical, intellectual, psychological, emotional, spiritual, sexual and social development of Gypsy traveller children living in a multiracial and diverse society. This understanding and insight have led to proper enquiries being made when assessing their welfare, health and education needs and has helped us guide and support access to appropriate and culturally sensitive services.

Local authorities have a duty under the Children Act 1989 regarding the welfare of 'children in need'. During WHEN assessments it is worth raising the issue of the vulnerability of Gypsy traveller children and reminding the local authority considering eviction that they have a 'duty of care' to the community. Accommodating the family is designed, as Cull and Roche (2001, p37), claim, to *help strengthen parenting capacity so they can respond to their children's needs in the long term*. It is therefore not set up to deal with Gypsy travellers' predicaments and, understandably, families would rather not become a 'social work case' when social work cannot resolve their long-term problem of homelessness.

Education, education, education

It has long been recognised in education, as Harrison-White (2002) states: *Traveller children...are the most severely deprived children in the country... Most of them do not go to school...and the children's needs are extreme and largely unmet* (p3). Kiddle (1999) says *provision for education has gradually developed and now 25% of children are on roll* (p265). Children on unauthorised encampments are protected by the Vulnerable Children's Admission Policy 2005, *where schools must take 5% over a full year group if the child is deemed vulnerable and that includes Traveller children* (Ryder, 2004, p1). Officers responsible for closing a site are now more aware through our WHEN assessments of the negative impact their actions have upon a child's educational development.

Valuing diversity

Often housing departments fail the community by offering 'housing'. Local authorities devoid of cultural sensitivity and their duty to supply accommodation (not housing) consider the status of homeless Gypsy travellers on unauthorised encampments as 'intentional' and at best offer under *the Housing Act 1996 an interim period in bed and breakfast* (Brayne and Carr, 2005, p717). Through WHEN assessments, we have been able to work with local authorities to consider fully what 'accommodation' means and in our local authority we have agreement that two families will remain until an alternative site can be found.

While the welfare, health and education status of Gypsy travellers has certain recognition and some needs are being met, the main concern for the community is still the intolerable living conditions on unauthorised sites. The law, as Thompson (2003) points out, *presents us with the potential to develop aspects of emancipatory practice* (p232). And Fawcett et al. (2004) maintain that *New Labour support children's rights to protection, economic support and social resources* (p161). However, I have not witnessed the state's responsibility to protect children from harm upheld when on unauthorised sites during evictions. In fact, any right to have a culturally stable home life has rarely been apparent.

This was evident when the basic needs of sanitation and waste disposal were refused. In an article published by the *West Briton* on 16 February 2006, the Chief Solicitor for Kerrier District Council said *the council would never have agreed to weekly removals of portaloos as this would have legitimised their presence*.

This view is one held by a number of local authorities and points to institutional racism. As the Macpherson Report (1999, p321), in Clements and Spinks (2003) describes:

> *It is incumbent on every institution to examine their policies and the outcome of their policies and practices to guard against disadvantaging any section of our communities.*

(p109)

The public perception

It is the views of the media and public institutions that inform the general public. Settled communities believe that minority ethnic groups are *a threat to a British way of life, they will take our jobs and housing and challenge the white British culture* (Spinks and Clements, 2003, p50). This is not the agenda of the Gypsy traveller community I work with: *The most disadvantaged group suffering the worst health inequalities of all groups in the UK* (DoH, 2004, p5) would just like equality of opportunity to a stable life.

The impact of Human Rights legislation

The European Convention on Human Rights was launched on 3 September 1953. The UK signed up to it but decided not to incorporate it into their legal system until the passing of the Human Rights Act 1998. It is hard to do justice to all the articles relevant to Gypsy travellers so I will concentrate on Article 8 to give a flavour of the Human Rights Act 1998's significance.

In the case of *Chapman* v *UK* the European Court of Human Rights 2001 (33 EHRR 18) held that a home set up without lawful authority could still be a 'home' within the terms of Article 8. Expanding on this, Johnson and Willers (2004) explain: *Article 8(1) has recently been interpreted as guaranteeing the right to respect for the traditional way of life for minorities* (p23). This demonstrates an understanding of the cultural need of Gypsy travellers to pursue their way of life even when living on unauthorised encampments.

This is further confirmed in the ODPM (2004) Guidance that informs *When a public authority is considering whether an interference with the right to respect for home and family life is 'necessary in a democratic society' they will have to ask themselves whether:*

i) there is a pressing social need for it; and

ii) it is proportionate to the aim pursued. (p4)

However, this is subject to justified limitations under Article 8 (2), as Johnson and Willers (2004) point out: *interference is necessary. . . in the service of other enumerated interests, including most relevantly. . . the protection of the environment for others' enjoyment* (p23).

Travellers' rights challenged by local community

This is an important point as often the rights of Gypsy travellers come into conflict with the rights of the local settled community. Protesters to enlarging a site in Cornwall claimed *the proposed extension would 'overdominate'. . . its 94 residents. . . it would lead to a loss of privacy. . . and deterioration in race relations* (*West Briton*, 5 July 2006).

It is therefore the concept of 'proportionality' on which a court must decide whether or not a violation is proportionate in the individual circumstances. This is particularly pertinent with regard to unauthorised encampments and the duty to carry out welfare enquiries. Now Willers (no date, p2) states *Public authorities need to ask themselves a number of questions before deciding whether to take eviction action*. And within my assessments I ask the local authority:

- Is the land the travellers are on inappropriate?

- If they are moved on, where will they go and are there any alternative temporary/ transit sites available?

- What provision of sites has the relevant local authority made for Gypsies and travellers in the area?

Thus it can be seen that the Human Rights Act 1998 has had the effect of broadening the scope of those matters that a public body ought to take into account before taking the steps of using eviction powers.

This Act coupled with the amended Race Relations Act 1976 (now 2000) has gone some way in further reminding public bodies that Gypsy travellers have rights too, and that:

> *a statutory general duty is placed upon public authorities to eliminate unlawful racial discrimination and to:*
>
> - *Promote equality of opportunity and good relations between people of different racial groups.*
> - *Devise a written policy for racial equality, monitoring and assessing its impact on minority ethnic group families and children and removing any disadvantage or discrimination.*
>
> (Lane and Ouseley, 2006, p1)

ACTIVITY 3.3

- *What does your local authority do well in meeting their general duty to promote equality of opportunity and good relations between different racial groups (Race Relations Act, s1) in relation to Gypsies and travellers?*

- *What could your local authority do differently to meet the above?*

Linking with universal policy

The Department for Education and Skills (2006) states that *the quality of life for minority ethnic families and children is to be genuinely improved . . . and equality issues are now central in contemporary national strategic documents such as 'Every Child Matters' and Excellence and Enjoyment* (p7). Inclusive policy along with the UN

Convention on the Rights of the Child 1989 inform practice. Lane and Ouseley (2006) go on to say:

> *by listening to children and ensuring their wellbeing ... we can secure the alignment of integration and enable personalised support for all children and their families in a way that matches their cultural needs and social and economic circumstances.*

(p3)

Kenrick and Clark in YWCA (2006) found that *although a harassed minority, travellers have not, in practice, had the protection which the law should afford to minorities* (p2).

> *Travellers are either all good or all bad to settled people, they don't see it might just be one family causing trouble.*

Young Person, Gypsy and Traveller Law Reform Coalition (G&TLRC)
Youth Conference 2005 in YWCA (2006, p2)

Practice overcoming discrimination

In practice Gypsies and travellers still seem to be on the verge of society, and criticising Gypsy travellers is still viewed by many as socially and legally acceptable.

The weight of prejudicial history and half-hearted state responses to the troubles faced by Gypsy travellers, make the attempts of our small dedicated team to raise a positive local profile for the community seem at times futile and overwhelming. As the CRE (2003) stated, *discrimination against Gypsies and Travellers is the last form of 'respectable' racism* (p9). Gypsy travellers are understandably disappointed and frustrated with agencies that seem to make few inroads to help them secure their homes and access services to specifically meet their needs.

We wax lyrical in social work about our understanding of, as Thompson (2001) describes, *the problems of minority ethnic groups who are subjected to oppression, degradation and discrimination* (p76) but with limited support and unsuitable resources, i.e. link into learning, play group, youth clubs, or accommodating their children, it is no surprise that Gypsy travellers tend not to seek social work help.

A balance needs to be struck, as Chapel (1993) warns, *there is always a danger that [a] service specifically designed for a minority group will not offer the range of provision available to the general population* (p5). My colleagues in health and education do not carry cases (except in extenuating circumstances) in an effort to bridge the gap between the community and mainstream services. In this way Chapel (1993) suggests: *specialist services aim to increase the knowledge and trust of Travellers empowering them to make full use of public care and educational services* (p5).

The limitations and frustrations

Over the past year I have felt burdened with the fact that while we have been able to help individuals to access health, social and educational services we seemed unable to help Gypsy travellers overcome the prevailing situation of homelessness.

Law and policy are still failing to prevent Gypsies and travellers from becoming homeless. Figures from the ODPM (2004) (now DCLG) indicate while *0.6% of the settled population are homeless, some 31% of the Gypsy Traveller population living in caravans or mobile homes do not have legal site accommodation* (p3).

It was therefore with great relief that we received the most recent DCLG Government Guidance. It outlines in circular 01/2006 Planning for Gypsy and Travellers Caravan Sites *guidance for local authorities on the planning aspects of finding sites for Gypsies and Travellers* (p1). The DCLG guidance finally (or again) tackles the problem of homelessness by placing a duty upon local authorities to provide sites for Gypsy traveller families. As Churcher (1996) states, *site provision is the key issue for the Travellers' lifestyle and health* (p26).

My local authority employed consultants in 2006 to undertake a Gypsies and travellers accommodation needs assessment, which subsequently quantified accommodation need across the county. I was part of the multi-agency steering group with representation from the Romany Gypsy, Irish heritage and new traveller communities. I was also a stakeholder and included in the interview process held predominantly by specifically employed members of the Gypsy traveller community.

New initiatives and optimism

It was with renewed vigour and enthusiasm that I embraced the new initiatives being undertaken by local authorities to meet one of the most fundamental rights of all human beings, the right to shelter. It is Maslow (1954) who informs us in his 'hierarchy of need' that if basic needs for food, water, shelter and clothing are not met, no human being can realise their full potential. It is therefore obvious that the welfare, health and educational disadvantages faced by Gypsies and traveller children and their families could be as a direct result of the fact that, as the YWCA (2006) explain: *the majority do not have a safe place to live, or travel to and from* (p3).

Restormel, a local borough council within Cornwall, was one of the first councils to produce their strategy and have stated that *Gypsy and Traveller communities should have the same access to decent and appropriate accommodation as every other resident and there should be sufficient sites available to meet their needs* (2007, p2). This is a great step forward and a commitment has been made by all local authorities to engage, as Restormel (2007) continues: *the Gypsy Traveller community, in a holistic manner, fully taking into consideration the views and aspirations of all members of the community* (p2). This is a welcome departure from recent research that states *ethnic minorities did not feel included and that consultation was generally poor* (O'Neale, 2000, p39).

This participatory model should ensure that there is no racial discrimination in the allocation of sites as all too often families have found themselves in the less desirable areas. Owusu-Bempah (2001) warns that *minority ethnic groups have had no choice but to live in deprived circumstances with their children, with all the concomitant paucity of services and facilities* (p46). By involving Gypsy travellers in the decision-making process, agencies have come some way in embracing social inclusion.

Inclusion and participation

Sure Start (2006) suggests *Inclusion is a process of identifying, understanding and breaking down barriers to participation and belonging* (p1). I work within a multi-agency team who understand the validity and who believe that inclusion as communicating directly with the Gypsy traveller community gives a clear insight into their cultural needs.

There have been few opportunities for Gypsy travellers to participate in public life; being forced to move on or having no secure address often makes it hard for Gypsy travellers to vote, let alone be heard when seeking assistance with welfare, health or education needs. Gypsy travellers often request the opportunity to make a contribution.

The YWCA (2006) spoke to young women who eloquently put it: *we have opinions on what matters to us; we are experts on our own lives* (p11). Real participation involves, as Sure Start (2006, p7) states, *along with talking to adults it means listening to children and recognising every person's equal entitlement to what's available with all barriers removed*. So if we have agreement to fully include the Gypsy traveller community in planning for their future we should be able to make a real difference to their deprived situation.

My assessments along with those of my colleagues have mirrored the national picture that the *general health of these marginalised families is poor* (Gerald, 1999, p11). Along with common problems associated with difficulty accessing permanent GP registration, no access to immunisation programmes or other health screening, more serious problems have also been uncovered. The high levels of *perinatal mortality, stillbirth and infant mortality* have a direct correlation with the *lack of access to health care, cultural insensitivity, and the horrifyingly poor environmental conditions in which some Travellers live* (Gerald, 1999, p11). Five years later the research carried out by the DoH (2004) demonstrated that little had changed. I do however believe that we are going to make inroads as our multi-agency partnership is working hard with the Gypsy traveller community to rectify this position.

Conclusion

The historical perspective shows us there has always been an uneasy relationship between Gypsy travellers and the settled community in the UK and there is deep-rooted and pervasive mistrust on both sides. Gypsy travellers have tended not to readily accept outsiders who, on the whole, have created laws and policies that have kept the community on the margins of the dominant population, and for too many years Gypsy travellers have been homeless, living in poverty, with little or no protection from prejudice and discrimination.

More recent laws and guidance have gone some way to help protect individuals within the community and brought about some humanitarian procedures and protocols that take greater notice of human rights. Children and vulnerable adults in the community are now dually considered as enquiries into their welfare, health and educational needs are assessed. This, in turn, reminds the public bodies of their duties and responsibilities to the Gypsy traveller community equitable to the settled community and that as a distinctive minority ethnic group their status affords them further rights to protection. It is therefore disappointing that despite this we still have a large proportion of Gypsy travellers living in deprivation and living on roadsides, in very poor conditions.

The most recent guidance has now put in place a duty on local authorities to provide sites. It is therefore the responsibility of all of us as voters to ensure this happens, and crucially that Gypsy travellers participate in the decision of where to place sites. This will finally ensure they have the same choices of where to live as is given to the settled community. Gypsy travellers do not want to take anything from the dominant settled population. They want to have a secure home, safe sites with sanitation and water supplies, and a way of life that enables them to be free from societal harassment and environmental problems. Welfare, health and education needs seem almost secondary to these more pressing ones, and I believe will only be achieved when a safe place to shelter is made available.

ACTIVITY **3.4**

- *How might the parental experience of education influence the Gypsy and traveller families' attitudes to schooling?*

- *What is the role of the virtual school in supporting educational progress of Gypsy and traveller children?*

- *At what age does the Gypsy family acknowledge the 'child' as an adult and how might this affect your approach?*

A student perspective of the law and social policy unit

The lives of the people we support and protect within social work are impacted upon enormously by the policy and legislation we work within. Any policy or law can only be as good as it is understood and implemented in practice. As social workers the responsibility lies with us to bring about improved outcomes and change using appropriately and creatively the duties and responsibilities we are empowered with.

The most helpful thing I found in undertaking the law unit was the chance to undertake research and analyse our findings together as a group. Getting away

$\rightarrow$

from the stress and demands of the workplace gave us a real opportunity to be able to bounce our experiences and ideas off one another. We were a diverse group from many different work bases, including social care, education, voluntary organisations and the military. Much of the legislation was universal but different people were experts in their own areas. This gave us real opportunity to expand each other's comfort zones in respect of where we operate most confidently and think more outside the box.

Of particular interest to me were the guest speakers. Listening to people with such vast knowledge and experience gave me the opportunity to look at things from a distance and more objectively. This can be very difficult in day-to-day practice where we so often have to be reactive, working under pressure and prioritising our workloads. At first I must confess that I was a little sceptical that some of the more academic speakers might be out of touch with the reality of practice. I was, however, pleasantly surprised at the empathy they could have and how pragmatic their talks could be. We very much shared our knowledge, skills and practice together. The barrister's lecture on human rights I found particularly interesting, and I think most of the group felt the same – a different professional's perspective was really helpful in informing our own practice.

The assignments, while challenging, were directly related to practice and very much reflected what we did on a day-to-day basis, in other words there were no trick questions, it even helped me at times to look more critically and reflectively at my own cases. There is no getting away from the fact, however, that the assignments do take a lot of commitment, which does involve some sacrifice but I enjoyed the ultimate sense of achievement. It also, in some respects, gave me more confidence in my knowledge base and how I was already applying law and policy effectively in my practice.

Legislation is changing so fast in modern child care practice it can be difficult to keep up, particularly since Every Child Matters. As social workers, many of us are also feeling more and more accountable for what we do and how we go about it. A more thorough and critical understanding of the law gives you more confidence to go about the job in a focused yet more relaxed way – more secure in your practice and feeling able to be more creative.

When you have a busy job and perhaps personal and family life, the thought of studying can at times feel daunting. There is no getting away from the fact that you do need a high level of self-motivation if you want to get the most out of the course. Much of the learning is also self-managed, and as boring as it sounds I found I had to be very organised to keep on top of everything. My wife and I also had our second child during the course and this did add to the pressure. The approach of the lecturers was very flexible and I did always feel treated with respect and understanding. As a group we also got to know one another and the atmosphere was very upbeat and friendly.

→

I was lucky to be in a supportive team with an encouraging line manager. This made a lot of difference to me and I do feel it is important for employers to support people through the course, in respect of both mentoring and with practical issues such as study time. After all, the aim is that practitioners will have increased their skills and knowledge by the end of the course. Whether or not you feel supported, however, you need to have a desire to do this course for yourself, and a belief that it will benefit your practice, perhaps your own career and most importantly the lives of those you work with.

Chapter 4

Evidence-based practice and managing the professional task

Contributors: Trevor Thomas, Denise Jackson and Andrew Chipangura

ACHIEVING A POST-QUALIFYING SPECIALIST AWARD IN CHILD CARE

This unit enabled the students to further explore social work theories and methods and integrate evidence-based research. It also examined adult learning theories and their application to social work practice.

The use of self in social work practice was also explored, including the emotional impact of direct work and the examination of personal beliefs and attitudes on judgement that influences their practice.

One of the primary aims of the unit was to ask students to critically evaluate an aspect of service delivery within their specialist field and demonstrate how services could be developed to improve outcomes for children. Students were also asked to reflect on their development as a social work practitioner.

A lecturer's perspective on the delivery of evidence-based practice and managing the professional task

This unit gave students the opportunity to provide a critical evaluation of an aspect of service delivery within their agency, and make proposals for service development that would have a direct impact in terms of improving outcomes for children and families who are users of these services. The task also required them to demonstrate their ability to enable the development of others.

Although the task had its limitations due to restricted timescales and management, this did not in any way inhibit the ideas and proposals the students wished to undertake. The majority of students clearly had views on some of the policy or practices that hindered positive working outcomes and innovative ideas of creating improved systems. These proposals for service development did not have any financial resources attached to them and had to be based on purely practical ways of managing change. Initially students were encouraged to discuss their proposals with their peers and benefited from constructive feedback on developing their proposals. Although some of the students worked in the same specialist area, the proposals for change were individual and examined a different aspect of service development.

→

The ranges of ideas were varied from introducing an induction programme to initiating mentoring projects within their organisation. The students were committed to 'making a difference' within their organisation and critically evaluating the impact this would have on their respective service user group.

The students strongly believed, with their social work experience and the benefit of the learning from the child care award, that they had developed knowledge and skills that they could share with their colleagues to enable the development of others and ultimately for the children and families they work with. They were eager to take on the challenges they had set themselves.

To enhance the learning experience, students were asked to present their proposal development to a senior manager within their agency, alongside their practice assessor. This was assessed as a direct observation as part of the Child Care Award requirements.

For many of the students this was a new challenge for them and many of them felt anxious about undertaking a presentation on an aspect of service development. Each student was given feedback not only on their presentation skills, but also on their proposal and development of their idea.

The final taught session required students to discuss their service development and to critically reflect on their personal learning. The students produced a catalogue of innovative and creative ideas for improving service delivery which was shared within their respective agencies. This showcased the work the students had undertaken and informed their colleagues/peers of new initiatives/developments within their organisations. Many of the developments are still continuing and have been adopted in other teams and authorities.

Teaching this unit demonstrated the innovative and creative abilities of the social work students and by providing them with an opportunity to impact on service delivery, I believe, ultimately enhanced outcomes for the children and young people they work alongside.

Service delivery to parents with learning disabilities – a critical appraisal

On 1 August 2004 social services in England embarked upon a process of change that led to the amalgamation of children's social services with Education (Batty, 2005). The Children Act 2004 promoted a wide range of reforms in order to strengthen the child protection system and give all young people the best start in life (Batty, 2005). It was argued that the integration of services to children would improve service delivery, meeting the needs of the most vulnerable children by focusing on preventative strategies rather than reactive intervention (Department for Education and Skills, 2005). The merger has had implications for social worker practitioners working with children and their parents, particularly when working with parents with learning disabilities.

The National Family and Parenting Institute has undertaken research into improving practice for this client group. Olson and Tyers (2004) found that good joint working between key agencies and social services teams is much needed, but insufficiently developed. It has been argued that joint working in this field will be further frustrated by the separation of social services adults' and children's teams (Ward, 2005). Parents with disabilities need access to services appropriate to their own individual needs, in order to ensure that their children receive optimal opportunities and improved life chances (McGaw and Newman, 2005). Practitioners recognise a significant shortfall in the understanding of colleagues from within social services and other agencies, with regard to how parents with learning disabilities are best supported in their parenting, particularly in relation to mother and baby placements. There appears to be a lack of awareness as to the learning styles and teaching methods that are most appropriate for this client group, thereby exacerbating the oppression and discrimination to which this client group is exposed (Macdonald, 2001).

The need for change

Drawing on experience in practice, discussion will focus upon how service delivery to parents with learning disabilities and their children can be improved, by enabling key workers to understand what works for parents with learning disabilities. Lest we forget, as practitioners we are accountable to service users, their carers, our professional body, our employing agency and statute. Social workers need to demonstrate that the human rights of both children and parents have been respected and considered, both in practice and in service provision (Brayne and Carr, 2003).

ACTIVITY *4.1*

- *Think of one thing that your agency does well in supporting parents with learning disabilities in their parenting role.*

- *Think of one thing your agency could do better in supporting parents with learning disabilities in their parenting role; what active role could you take in promoting this change?*

RESEARCH SUMMARY

Research has shown that local authorities are beginning to give greater respect to the parental rights of parents with disabilities (Olson and Tyers, 2004). However Olson and Tyers (2004) found that practitioners often report a lack of confidence in supporting this client group, due to confusion as to whether appropriate support comes under the remit of adult services or children's services. It could be argued that this confusion has been exacerbated by the recent separation of adults' and children's social services departments (Ward, 2005). However, this lack of confidence and confusion mirrors the pressures of high caseloads and budget constraints (Kidner, 2002). Unfortunately, for parents with learning disabilities, the reality is that when they come to the attention of children's

→

services, they are more likely to have their children taken into care than any other client group (Macdonald, 2001). Historically, there has been extensive ethical, moral and legal debate as to whether it is appropriate for people with learning difficulties to live in the community, to enjoy sexual fulfilment and to become parents (Bambrick and Roberts, 1990; Green and Paul, 1974; Hall, 1975: Hertz, 1979, cited in McGaw and Newman, 2005, p1).

Practitioners need to be imaginative and innovative, to ensure that families that include parents with learning difficulties receive a multi-agency service that will be appropriate and conducive to their needs (Olson and Tyers, 2004). Researchers recommend that when working with children whose parents have learning disabilities, professionals need to view their parents in the same way as non-disabled parents (Olson and Tyers, 2004). McGaw and Newman (2005) argue that parental rights and children's welfare are best supported through the combination of positive attitudes and evidence-based practice. As with the majority of parents, parents with learning disabilities want to parent their children well. Unfortunately, with regard to service provision, there appears to be a one-size-fits-all policy and inter-agency collaboration and sustainable service provision is continually influenced by cost effectiveness, budget constraints and human resources (Olson and Tyers, 2004). It seems that these issues will continue to be a barrier as the recent reorganisation of children's services has not been supported with additional funding and this will inevitably impact upon sound evidence-based preventative services (Ahmed, 2005).

Budget implications

Obstructions to inter-agency practice and frustration with regard to budgetary constraints can be exacerbated due to a lack of understanding and awareness of parents' learning needs; this can result in inappropriate, unrealistic expectations. All parents need support with their parenting at some stage; however, research suggests that for parents with learning disabilities full attention needs to be given to identifying and meeting parental support needs (Olson and Tyers, 2004). An inter-agency plan is considered crucial as it can identify who is best suited to assess and support a family (McGaw and Newman, 2005).

June (a 10-month-old baby) and her mother (who has a learning disability) were placed in a mother and baby placement to offer a nurturing environment where June's mother would receive the appropriate guidance and support necessary to enable her to adequately parent June. However, the efficiency of the plan depended upon the workers being aware of June's mother's learning needs, her style of learning and what methods were appropriate to meet these needs. Research undertaken by McConnell et al. (1997, cited in McGaw and Newman, 2005) from interviews with 40 parents with learning

→

CASE STUDY *continued*

disabilities, found that interventions with this client group needed to be done with their participation and based upon the specific learning needs of parents. On reflection, it could be argued that June and her mother were in an unfavourable environment, one that was not conducive to June's mother's learning.

McGaw and Newman (2005) suggest that there is a consensus of opinion that parents with learning disabilities are best supported within their home environment. Unfortunately for June's mother, home-based support was not considered an option, due to the breakdown of a relationship which left both herself and June homeless. June's mother's learning and support needs were identified through assessment conducted by the Special Parenting Service. Subsequently, models and methods were devised for meeting those needs. However, in order to meet their needs effectively, a commitment was needed by all the professionals involved to be open to June's mother's learning needs and to be proactive in supporting her (Olson and Tyers, 2004). June's mother suffered a considerable amount of neglect, abuse and deprivation as a child, which exacerbated the effects of her learning disability upon her parenting capacity (Macdonald, 2001).

Researchers such as Polanski et al. (1985, cited in Macdonald, 2001) have highlighted a correlation between neglectful parents having poor parenting histories. It can therefore be argued that, until the needs of neglectful parents are met, it may prove difficult to improve their responsiveness to their children. However, for June's mother, this was not the case; some of the key people involved in the support package, including the foster carers, became frustrated with the pace of her ability to learn. It became increasingly obvious that there was a distinct lack of understanding on the foster carers' behalf as to how June's mother's learning disability and her previous childhood experiences impacted upon her ability to put into practice the advice and guidance given to her. The success of any support package in these circumstances is dependent on the openness and attitude of the staff involved and the quality of professional knowledge regarding the ability to match the intervention needed to the abilities of the parent (McGaw and Newman, 2005).

On reflection, it seemed that the inadequacies in the support package and subsequent plan of intervention, were due to the lack of professional training that exists in the UK with regards to how best to support this service user group (McGaw and Newman, 2005). In order to support this client group effectively, Crittenden (1993, 1999 cited in Macdonald, 2001, p71) suggests taking an eclectic approach, e.g. by integrating types of theories and models that inform social work practice. These include: attachment theory, learning theory and cognitive psychology. Environmental factors also need to be considered; it is recognised that when undertaking work with parents with learning difficulties, taking an ecological approach is essential (Macdonald, 2001).

The Special Parenting Service uses the nationally validated *Parenting Assessment Manual* as an assessment tool for parents with learning disabilities (McGaw et al., 1999 cited in McGaw and Newman, 2005, p30). The manual is believed to provide a holistic, functional tool, which assesses vulnerable parents and their children from birth to

19 years of age. The manual encapsulates materials, pictures and terminology that have been meticulously collated to match the needs of vulnerable parents and are designed to be user-friendly across agencies (McGaw and Newman, 2005). The assessment tool also incorporates the use of information technology to enhance service delivery. For example, the Parenting Assessment Manual software allows access to an electronic child and parent profile to facilitate programme planning; it also provides a risk-assessment tool to identify health and safety factors within the family (South Coast Solutions, 2004).

Adults with learning disabilities

It is important to remember when working with adults with learning disabilities that many of the general characteristics associated with adult learners are not necessarily as prevalent (McGaw and Newman, 2005). For example, the concept that adult learners have the ability to make balanced judgements about themselves and others (Rogers, 2004) may not necessarily be the case with regard to adults with learning disabilities, therefore they are vulnerable to being undervalued and exploited (Corby, 2000). Rogers (2004) criticises behavioural, cognitive and humanist adult learning theories; he argues that they make sweeping generalisations about adult learning which cannot always be justified. This is due, in part, to the theories' failure to allow for the diversity of human responses. It is also argued that many learning theories are decidedly Western and that they fail to take account of the oppression and exclusion that women are exposed to in today's society (Rogers, 2004). This highlights the need for the support package for June's mother to reflect her learning needs (Macdonald, 2001).

ACTIVITY **4.2**

- *How do you ensure that Article 8 of the European Convention of Human Rights is accounted for within your practice?*
- *How is this evidenced within your written records?*

The public perception

It is argued that the child care practice of parents with learning difficulties is more open to scrutiny by statutory agencies than that of those parents who do not have learning disabilities or difficulties (Corby, 2000). Parents with learning disabilities are often viewed by other professionals and key workers as being a homogenous group with similar characteristics (Corby, 2000). However, on reflection, such attitudes may be due to the research in this field. Attempts to measure the effectiveness of interventions with regard to parents with learning difficulties are often frustrated, due to methodological issues such as: identification of parents with learning disabilities, socio-economic, demographic reasons and the recruitment of parents who are already known to the statutory agencies and therefore not representative of the population as a whole (McGaw and Newman, 2005). Some research studies simply highlight the correlation between low intelligence and child abuse, even though it is recognised that research demonstrating the circumstances in which inadequate parenting can lead to significant harm is more useful (Corby, 2000). Furthermore, attention needs to paid to the situations of parents with learning difficulties from different cultural and ethnic groups (O'Hara and Martin, 2003, cited in McGaw and Newman, 2005, p71). Nevertheless, with regard to June and her mother, all the above appear to be conducive to the negativity regarding the likely success of their mother and baby placement.

Inconsistencies regarding service delivery to parents with disabilities have been identified (Olson and Tyers, 2004); these are reflected in the need to be proactive to ensure that June and her mother receive an appropriate service, i.e. one that is conducive to their needs. Failure to do so would be a breach of both June's and her mother's human rights with regard to Article 8 of the Human Rights Act 1998 (Brayne and Carr, 2003). Furthermore, it would be in violation of the Codes of Practice for social care workers (GSCC, 2002), i.e. as a social worker there is a requirement to *protect the rights and promote the interests of service users and their carers*. Olson and Tyers (2004) identified a need to improve communication and inter-agency working between adults' and children's social services teams along with other key agencies such as health education and leisure, in order to improve service delivery to parents with disabilities.

Ethical dilemmas

When working with such complex situations, a social worker should retain sight of the service user, social work values, responsibility and accountability (Lishman, 1998); quite often these elements conflict, resulting in many an ethical dilemma (Banks, 2001). A social worker must balance the rights of the service user with their duty to their employing agency (Banks, 2001). For example, when working with parents with learning difficulties it is never acceptable to promote the interests of the parents over those of the child (McGaw and Newman, 2005). However, each parent's parenting capacity is subject to assessment and it is rarely possible to promote the welfare of children without also promoting the welfare of the significant adults in their lives (Macdonald, 2001). There can be dilemmas relating to resources and the best interests of the child are arguably overridden due to budget constraints (Olson and Tyers, 2004).

Although social work practice with children and families is now adopting a more preventative approach, managers have to consider cost implications when funding preventative practices (Macdonald, 2001) this is despite research that suggests that costs are repaid over time due to reduced use of other social care associated services (Newman, 2002). Many social care services perceive themselves as insufficiently well equipped to deliver a service to this client group (McGaw and Newman, 2005). However, cost of provision does not appear to be such a constraint with regard to the cost of issuing care proceedings, or when services are needed to enable a child to remain in substitute care (Mason et al., 1997).

When faced with such dilemmas it is necessary for a social worker to be reflective and examine their own beliefs and value base and thereby assess how these are impacting upon their judgement and practice (Banks, 2001). Social workers can experience frustration when having to balance meeting the needs of the child and their carers and negligence and the burden of administrative accountability; these are all stress factors that, if they go unrecognised and unsupported, can lead to a worker's subsequent ill health and errors in judgement (Thorne, 1997). Regular supervision for all social workers is essential and is a process with more dimensions than purely case management (Banks, 2001). Supervision can promote reflection, providing a social worker with the opportunity to reflect on personal beliefs, values, dilemmas, and professional departmental issues (Kidner, 2002). Furthermore, good supervision offers the opportunity to apply current research and theory to their practice (Kidner, 2002), thereby facilitating the learning process (Carroll, 2001) and the effective use of evidence-based practice (Olson and Tyers, 2004). It is recognised that parents with learning disabilities are among the poorest and most underprivileged families in British society (McGaw and Newman, 2005). The work involved with this client group is demanding, the emotional impact is considerable, and stress factors are high for service users and social workers (Banks, 2001).

According to Olson and Tyers (2004), the knowledge of managers, key workers and colleagues, regarding how best to support parents with disabilities, appears to be patchy and somewhat uninformed; they highlight the importance of culturally appropriate training for key frontline staff in disability issues, along with the skills necessary to communicate effectively with parents. Tymchuck (1992b, cited McGaw and Newman, 2005, p66) found that the openness of staff, attitudes and the quality of professional skills and knowledge and especially the need to match intervention to the characteristics of parents, were among the main predictors of adequate learning for parents with learning disabilities.

Improving service outcomes

In order to improve service provision for June and her mother, regular informal reviews were held at the mother and baby placement. This gave the foster carers the opportunity to discuss the learning and support needs of both June and her mother with a representative from the Special Parenting Service who specialises with this client group. Since its inception in my local authority in 1988, the Special Parenting Service has seen more than 850 families in which one or both parents have a learning disability; this is out of a total population of some 500,000 (McGaw and Newman, 2005, p7). The informal reviews enabled the carers and other key workers to understand the complexities of linking impairment to parenting. The reviews facilitated workers to recognise that disablement is not a homogenous entity, that different kinds of impairment may present different types of challenges towards parents which require different packages of tailored support (McGaw and Newman, 2005). The reviews promoted learning and partnership between June's mother and the workers involved, which provided a forum that was conducive to strategic medium-term planning. Information was shared with June's mother regarding how available resources could be used in order to achieve common goals, e.g. June's mother having the opportunity to learn the skills necessary to enhance her parenting capacity and in doing so improve future outcomes for June (Hudson, 2000). These reviews helped to manage existing and potential conflict, by creating an atmosphere of partnership, clarity, tolerance and openness that challenged stereotypical approaches regarding service delivery to June and her mother (Brechin, 2000).

Good practice dictates that a social worker should challenge assumptions, stereotypes, oppression and discrimination (Thompson, 1997). There is also a requirement that a social worker contributes to the learning and development of others and promotes good practice (GSCC, 2002). On reflection, team meetings and team away-days provided a means to share positive experiences relating to the informal reviews of June and her mother's placement. It was then proposed that regular informal reviews of mother and baby placements should be considered as part of the organisational service development to improve outcomes for both children and their parents. Team meetings and away-days also provided the opportunity to address some of the issues raised during my involvement with June and her mother relating to the inadequacy of professional knowledge in relation to service provision to parents with learning disabilities (McGaw and Newman, 2005). This was undertaken by inviting representatives from the Special Parenting Service to meet with colleagues and support staff, including social workers from the Community Care team. A psychologist from the Special Parenting Service presented theories relating to evidence-based good practice and learning techniques; for example, models and methods used to engage parents, possible strategies for responding to parents' diverse learning needs such as promoting the use of visual aids and parenting skill cards, both of which are beneficial to parents with learning difficulties who find reading difficult (McGaw and Newman, 2005).

Working together

Regular meetings with other agencies such as the local health visitors also proved conducive in enabling me to share knowledge and experience and, equally importantly, to listen to the experiences of other agencies regarding service delivery to parents with learning disabilities. A multidisciplinary approach is considered essential to improve service delivery and thereby promote optimal outcomes for children (Cotson et al., 2001). Furthermore, it is argued that the informal training that takes place while working together on the front line can be just as informative to practice and service delivery as formal training (Cameron and Lart, 2003).

The recognition that service delivery can be improved by the closer working together of social care agencies is supported in the Every Child Matters initiative, for example, by the planned implementation of the Common Assessment Framework (DfES, 2005) and Integrated Children's System (ICS) (DfES, 2005). The ICS is underpinned by information technology and takes into account the structure of the Common Assessment Framework (CAF) in order that the exchange of information between the two can be facilitated and in turn assist managers and practitioners in social services to improve outcomes for children in need and their families (DfES, 2005). There are benefits in having the ICS in terms of service provision, e.g. having a national information technology system capable of monitoring a child's educational attainment, placement stability, social services involvement and family members and others who are significant in a young person's life (DfES, 2005).

The introduction of the ICS reinforces that social workers and their managers are accountable for meeting targets, e.g. timed assessments and less concern about the quality and nature of service provision to service users (Brayne and Carr, 2003). There needs to be an emphasis on the quality of recording on a child's file, e.g. actions taken or reasons for inaction, the decision-making process, including managerial decisions and supervision notes (Brayne and Carr, 2003). On reflection, this is of particular relevance when there is conflict, for example, when a worker disagrees with a management decision. Brayne and Carr (2003) noted that courts are increasingly holding local authorities responsible for their employees' mistakes. Lord Laming (2003) highlighted that the resulting risk to social workers was greater than the risk to senior managers. This is supported by an article in *Community Care* (2005), which stated that the Haringey Council chief executive criticised in Lord Laming's inquiry (2003) is set to receive an unconfirmed early retirement package in the region of one million pounds; in contrast, the social worker involved in the case has had to fight for her rights and faces less favourable prospects in the future. Therefore, it seems essential to me that when conflict arises in such circumstances a social worker needs to ensure that they are working from a sound knowledge base of practice, policy and research and that their recording is clear regarding the decisions made and actions taken.

Conclusion

The proposals for improving organisational service delivery to parents with learning disabilities and promoting improved outcomes for their children may not appear to be conducive to the culture of performance management. Many parenting programmes for this service user group will be long-term provision and need to be funded as such to meet the objective that parents and children should, ideally, remain together (McGaw and Newman, 2005). In my experience managers are often reluctant to release funds for longer-term packages of care for this service user group, often using arguments such as *they will become dependent, you are setting them up to fail, we must consider the cost*, instead preferring time-limited intervention despite evidence that longer-term intervention is cost effective (Macdonald, 2001). It seems unrealistic to expect families who have long histories of cumulative problems and disadvantage should overcome the myriad of problems, discrimination, disadvantage and oppression that they face in a matter of weeks (Macdonald, 2001). In their research Olson and Tyers (2004) found that several managers who were responsible for strategic decision-making in relation to parents with disabilities, stated the introduction of a performance indicator relating to the support of parents with disabilities would help galvanise support to this client group. This supports the argument that, in a performance culture, if it does not get measured, it does not get done (Olson and Tyers, 2004). Although valued support can involve substantial packages of support, there is research that shows that low-cost, imaginative solutions devised in partnership with parents are equally as valuable (Olson and Tyers, 2004).

Unfortunately, it has been my experience that both nationally and locally, service delivery to parents with learning disabilities is fragmented. Although many of the old prejudices appear to have diminished, parents with disabilities are often supported by social care staff including managers, social workers, foster carers and health visitors, who doubt the parents' ability to parent adequately (McGaw and Newman, 2005); this points to the need for further training regarding this particular service user group. Unfortunately, national professional training in this field is sparse. Some would argue that this is due to there being no national strategy on assessment training and service development; much of the support nationally for parents with learning disabilities is passed to other voluntary or non-statutory agencies. Tymchuck (1999, cited in McGaw and Newman, 2005, p70) identified the need for support for parents with learning difficulties to rest with mainstream services, supported by the voluntary sector rather than vice versa.

A child of a parent with a disability does not necessarily equate to a child in need (Olson and Tyers, 2004). My proposals for improved service delivery for parents with learning disabilities, such as regular informal reviews for those parents placed in mother and baby placements and for frontline workers to be given training on the learning needs and styles of adults with learning disabilities, could improve outcomes for children and families. However, there also needs to be a shift in local managerial policy for any developments with regard to service provision to parents with learning disabilities to be sustained. Support packages to this client group are often long term and will need funding as such; they cannot be static and will need to change in order to meet the developmental needs of the child and the associated learning requirements of the parent (McGaw and Newman, 2005). It could be argued that the current emphasis on preventative services might support this proposal (DfES, 2005). Nevertheless, there remains a need for social workers to be proactive in contributing to the learning of others and to do this in partnership with their employer. Employers must abide by the Code of Practice for Employers of Social Care Workers (GSCC, 2002) and therefore provide opportunities for development and training, in order to enable frontline staff to develop and strengthen their skills and knowledge and thereby ensure that anti-oppressive and anti-discriminatory practice are more than just rhetoric (Thompson, 1997).

ACTIVITY **4.3**

- *What does current research into parent training programmes for parents with leaning disabilities tell us?*

- *Are these research findings reflected in your practice?*

SCIE research briefing 14: Helping parents with learning disabilities in their role as parents (published February 2005) www.scie.org.uk/publications/briefings/briefing14/index.asp

A student's perspective on the evidence-based practice and managing the professional task unit

I qualified as a social worker abroad several years ago and am undertaking the Post-Qualifying Child Care Specialist Award, the first training I have been able to access. My social work training and subsequent practice in the country I trained in was generic. Coming to the United Kingdom made me feel out of my depth due to the different social, cultural and legal landscape. This is hardly surprising as the guiding principle seemed to be the assumption that social work practice is universal and its application therefore needed little or no adjustment regarding those incoming foreign-trained practitioners. Yet the cross-cultural universality of social work values is in reality a myth, although there are many basic methods, processes and values which do underpin the practice and hence transcend cultural barriers.

Undertaking the evidence-based practice and managing the professional task unit gave me the opportunity to examine myself within the agency and highlighted to me the lack of induction I received as a newcomer to UK social work. Having the opportunity to develop an 'induction' training programme that could focus on some of the key issues for internationally trained social workers was an exciting prospect. The induction package was intended to identify multiple challenges usually faced by the social workers entering UK social work. These included aspects of racial discrimination, language skills, culture, etc. It addressed how social workers need to be exposed to new systems of thinking, new value systems, new cultures and new views of the world. It has also provided the extent to which social workers have had to contend with changing management structures, changing client needs, organisational structures and working practices, including terminologies.

To really imbed the induction training I needed to engage my local authority's training department, so I could work with them, to ensure the package was fit for purpose and feasible. The training department had already recognised a need to develop such an induction package and although they had an international recruitment strategy, they had not developed an international induction programme to support the strategy. This had resulted in a number of internationally recruited social workers leaving the local authority within a six-month period. This had major financial costs to the agency in which I work. The induction programme allowed me to meet a variety of staff within my organisation that I had never come across before and we were able to discuss issues that had impacted on my own personal transition to UK social work. I found the organisation very receptive to developing this induction package. Although the service development took time to develop, it has now been rolled out across the large authority in which I work and has been delivered to over 20 internationally recruited staff. The feedback from this development has been received very positively and I have become a mentor to some of the new staff entering UK social work.

Without the input of this unit I do not believe I would ever have been able to develop this induction package or become a resource to the organisation in

→

which I work. I now feel respected for the knowledge I have in my area of practice and personal experience which I believe is valued. The training on this unit has helped me to be more critically analytical in my practice. I have been able to apply evidence-based research in my everyday practice which I have no doubt enhanced the outcomes for the children and their families I work with.

This unit has given me confidence in the manner in which I discharge my duties. This was a very positive development and this also earned me respect among my workmates and service users. It is therefore hoped that this contribution will stimulate debate as social work evolves to meet new and ever-changing circumstances. I am now contributing at a national level to the recruitment of international social work staff.

Managing and supporting young people with sexually harmful behaviour

Introduction

Between a quarter and a third of all cases of sexual abuse in the UK involve children and young people as perpetrators (Hackett, 2005). A significant amount has been learnt over the past 10 years about the pathways to offending and the needs of this group of young people, but policy and practice responses are still very variable. Cornwall has achieved a great deal in terms of developing a co-ordinated framework for a multi-agency service for children and young people with sexually harmful behaviour, in line with the *Working Together to Safeguard Children* guidance (Department of Health, 1999, updated 2006). The Local Safeguarding Board used their powers to pool funds from key partner agencies, namely Social Care, Youth Offending Team and Partnership Services for Children and Families to set up the local Risk Assessment and Management Support Team. Detailed guidance has been drawn up and implemented within Cornwall's Child Protection Procedures to ensure a multi-agency response that provides a care plan for every young person. In addition to this, there is an adopted protocol in place with the police to ensure that appropriate emphasis is placed, following careful assessment to judge levels of risk. This in turn informs whether a young person is able to stay within his/her own family, or requires substitute care and, if so, to what extent the young person needs to be supervised.

Risk management

The principle of risk management should form the basis of a care plan to support a young person in the community and is the foremost tool to address the regulation of the young person's sexually harmful behaviours. Risk management is distinct from safe care in the way that the professionals and the carers engage actively with the child or young person to discuss his/her sexually harmful behaviour, to plan strategies for supervision and to enable ways for the child or young person to demonstrate he/she can take responsibility. Safe care is the framework of boundaries in place within a home or residential environment to ensure privacy, respect for others and appropriate interactions.

Placement provision

The issue of placement provision for those children and young people who are unable to remain at home, or who are removed from home as a result of their offending behaviour, has never been afforded due scrutiny. Substitute care provision in Cornwall for children and young people with sexually harmful behaviour is patchy, inconsistent, inadequately resourced for the task they face and lacks a co-ordinated strategic response. Issues that prevent placements being made available include financial pressures; the fact that taking a child or young person with high supervision needs prevents the carer from having other placements, thereby reducing their income; lack of detailed background information; lack of training and support; and lack of therapeutic input for the child. These are all factors cited by carers as deterrents. The National Standards for Foster Care was published six years ago, recommending that each authority *should carry out an audit of its foster care services – identify where there are shortfalls in provisions and specify how it will plan to address these* (Recommendation 14, UK Joint Working Party on Foster Care Report and Recommendations, 1999). There is no specific recruitment or training to ensure that appropriate carers, with sufficient experience and skills, are adequately prepared and supported to undertake the complex task of caring for a child or young person with sexually harmful behaviours although there is a tacit acknowledgement that this should be incorporated in future service plans.

Prior to 2002 and the inception of the Risk Assessment and Management Support Team, children and young people with sexually harmful behaviour were placed in specialist residential resources out of county. The remit for the Risk Assessment and Management Support Team initially was to work with the county residential services to enable the majority of these young people to remain accommodated in or near to their local community. Training on safe care and managing risk was central to developing this provision.

What was clearly evident from the Health of Children in Care training day was that those foster carers who had previously received training and support from the Risk Assessment and Management Support Team were more knowledgeable about the distinction between 'safe care' and 'risk management' and were able to articulate a proactive stance that supported the view that children and young people with sexually harmful behaviour could be managed effectively within a family environment. This includes young people subject to registration (Sex Offenders Act 1997 and Sexual Offences Act 2003).

ACTIVITY **4.5**

- *Find out what provision exists in your area to manage and support young people with sexually harmful behaviour.*

- *What might be the dilemmas for staff working with young people who may be both victims and perpetrators?*

RESEARCH SUMMARY

In spite of the high levels of concern among professionals about how best to manage children and young people with sexually harmful behaviour, there has been little research with regard to foster placement. Farmer and Pollock's (1998) study found that those children who had been abused and those with sexually harmful behaviour in foster care were more likely to have been placed at some time on the Child Protection Register (under any category), to have had a previous care experience and to have spent longer in care than their non-abused counterparts. They were more likely to have had severe educational problems and to have experienced rejection and disrupted parenting, i.e. multiple separations from their main parent, a parent who had multiple partners, and care which adversely affected their emotional development. Clearly these are some of the most damaged and vulnerable children and young people in the care system, warranting specialist skilled intervention and care. Farmer and Pollock also identified that in spite of the risks there was a tendency for care givers to normalise the sexual behaviours and to develop high thresholds before action was taken (1998, p44). Hackett, Masson and Phillips (2003) identify that the most significant gaps in service provision across the UK for this group of children and young people are local appropriate placements and a trained foster care service.

The Health of Children in Care training day keynote speech announced the county's Safe Care initiative and how this would be in the format of a written document as part of the placement agreement for each new foster placement. This is in line with Standard 2.7, *The child's assessment is used to inform care plans, placement agreements, reviews,* and Standard 2.6, *Copies of the assessment are given to the child (unless deemed inappropriate), the family, the foster carer and anyone else involved in the child's protection and development* (UK National Standards in Foster Care, 1999).

The workshop format

The workshop format that I presented afforded opportunities for individuals to put their questions and observations. There was a certain amount of taught material that needed to be presented, in order to have sufficient common information to facilitate meaningful discussion. Participants were from diverse backgrounds and professional disciplines and I had no advance knowledge of this. I chose to establish group identity with a show of hands. I also needed to know how many of the participants had prior knowledge of the work of the Risk Assessment and Management Support Team. This enabled me to deliver appropriate information that could meet their learning needs. I presented the taught material to the participants using PowerPoint so that participants received both aural and visual stimulus, as people assimilate information in differing ways. In order to cope with the time constraints imposed I had written a reference manual on the subject (managing risk) as I knew I could not effectively 'teach' the skills required in the time available. I identified three key points that I wanted participants to leave with; everything else I said could be read about later in the manual.

- What do the risk assessment and management support team do?

- What is risk management?

- How is this different from safe care?

Taking account of learning styles

With reference to the principles regarding the characteristics of adult learners (Knowles, 1990), I wanted to create time for questions and discussion because the participants needed to be respected as mature, motivated and self-directed learners. There would be a range of experience within the room that I could draw upon and use this pre-existing knowledge to inform others. People often learn more effectively from conversation with fellow participants. I chose to abandon a case study discussion in preference to a problem-solving discussion as not only was this the best use of the time available, but I noted from the questions from the floor during the keynote address that participants were keen to seek out solutions to the issues being presented in their day-to-day experience. Significant points were written on a flipchart so that key themes and messages that would be useful to their daily caring situations could be reinforced.

Participants were given pamphlets on internet abuse (Home Office, 2004) and guidance on how to be more IT literate so that they could monitor online chatrooms and review their child's internet access record. This was singled out as a subject in its own right because people have many anxieties about regulating children on the internet. There was no opportunity to discuss this in detail, but I wanted participants to have a tool to go away with that could be supportive and aid decision-making within the home. The leaflet gave several web addresses for further detailed information for parents and carers to access.

Each workshop subject merited a training day of its own. We were aware of this, but decided to go ahead because there are limitations to foster carers' availability. To a certain extent it was experimental, as it is the first joint training initiative of this kind for foster carers. There will be an opportunity to formally review the day as a group of presenters and organisers at a later date.

Student evaluation

My evaluation of the day is that, despite it being overly ambitious, there was still value to organising it as it was, because it enabled participants to have a comprehensive overview of the sexual health needs of the children and young people in their care. It flagged up the importance of sexual development, sexual identity, safe care, management of risk and sex education for children and young people in the care system (Standards 6.12, 6.13 and 7.10). These are problematic issues for carers and professionals alike and are often pushed to the back burner.

What was evident from the group of carers that attended this training day was the extent to which they wanted these issues to be seen as a priority and how much they welcomed frank discussion. It would be reasonable to assume that the group is not representative of the carer group in its entirety and that this group are the most proactive and motivated to learn about this issue as demonstrated by their having chosen to attend. A study by ADSS in 1997 revealed that only 16 per cent of carers reported they always attended training, although 56 per cent felt training was relevant sometimes; 53 per cent thought strongly that training should be made ongoing and compulsory. To obtain a comprehensive understanding of need, then, those carers who didn't attend need to be canvassed and non-attendance due to practical difficulties, low priority, motivation, lack of confidence and perception of relevance should be checked out.

Whatever their reason for attending, it was clear from those present that they were committed to providing a better service for the children and young people they had placed with them. Research indicates that carers who felt prepared for the specific task to meet a child's individual needs were less likely to say they found the child more difficult than they expected, or that they felt like giving up (Treseliotis et al., 1999). Debate exists as to whether post-approval training should be mandatory for foster carers, but it is advocated strongly that carers living with children and young people with sexually harmful behaviours must have sufficient knowledge and skills to meet their needs. Hackett (2001) identifies that the general shortage of appropriate community-based placement options often militates against an effective intervention response, even if therapeutic provision is available locally.

Learning outcomes

Key learning points obtained from the carers on the training day were: the need for comprehensive information, clear care plans, safe care and risk management plans prior to placement, therapeutic support for the child and access to professionals who can give advice and guidance. Discussion in the workshop identified that there is a distinction between safe care and risk management, and that, while the two are not mutually exclusive, both are necessary if the young person is going to be managed within a home environment. This learning needs to be taken forward with the foster care service for inclusion in the policy document on safe care and incorporated within the safe care initiative. The carers recognised that they needed to be actively addressing the issues with the young person, as well as with the professional support network.

The participants appeared to accept that the needs of this group of children and young people are not fundamentally different from those of other young people who have problems. Clearly, there are carers within the fostering service who are willing to assist young people in the process of moving away from patterns of sexually abusive behaviour, towards developmentally appropriate and healthy forms of sexual expression, if they can access the appropriate support to assist them in this task. To a certain extent the Risk Assessment and Management Support Team already had evidence of this from our experience of the small group of carers that we had been supporting over the previous three years and who are successfully managing young people within their home and local community.

There are several learning points from this training day that may contribute to proposals for service development. I am fortunate to hold a developmental post that has a county-wide remit to promote the needs of children and young people with sexually harmful behaviour. As in all organisations, there are some individuals and groups who are more resistant to change than others. The Commission for Social Care Inspectorate report (February 2005) on the county's fostering service opened the door to change and this is evidenced by, among other things, the introduction of placement agreements, the safe care initiative (and policy) and renewing the membership to the British Agency for Adoption and Fostering (BAAF), thereby accessing practice guidance on standards and training for carers. There is a spirit of openness now that is receptive to ideas from outside the fostering service and as such I would propose the following to contribute toward service development and thereby have an impact on improving outcomes for children and their families.

1. The collaboration with the other presenters of the training has established a foundation for a co-ordinated approach to working with this group of children and young people. I have greater confidence that carers in the future will receive a response that is congruent with the Risk Assessment and Management Support Team ethos and that we now share a common definition of safe care and risk management. This can be built upon by further training days to reach a wider circle of carers.

2. The co-ordination of the training day with the Foster Care Services' introduction of their safe care initiative was very useful. This increases the opportunity to develop common terminology and common agreement on care standards. The safe care initiative is an ideal starting point for discussion about incorporating principles of risk management for all carers and establishing a baseline standard of care. This may lay a foundation for more carers being better prepared to care for children and young people with sexually harmful behaviours, particularly as this initiative will be delivered to newly recruited carers within their preparation training 'Choosing to foster'.

3. The Risk Assessment and Management Support Team could provide input to foster carers' preparation training groups on a rolling programme and help carers become familiar with the county's resource for children and young people with sexually harmful behaviour; they could learn about the needs of this population and learn about the

multi-agency child protection system that supports them. This might place a heavy burden on the Risk Assessment and Management Support Team, in which case an alternative strategy would be to write the training material to be incorporated within the 'Choosing to foster' course, and train the trainers to deliver it. Closer links and improved collaboration could result, as members of the fostering training team would need to know background information about the Risk Assessment and Management Support Team in order to answer questions from participants.

4. Foster carers are already involved in cascading training to newly recruited carers. The practicalities of implementing a risk-management programme could best be communicated by someone who has had experience of living it. I had thought of involving a carer with the workshop that I presented this time but the time constraint of 45 minutes prevented me from doing it. In the future if the training is organised in such a way as to afford more time, I would like to reconsider this.

5. A range of community-based welfare-oriented resources are needed for children and young people with sexually harmful behaviour. We have successfully maintained the majority of children and young people in-county, with very limited recourse to specialist out-of-county residential placements. Wherever possible, young people receive support in small residential establishments shared with one other resident. This is a costly and finite resource that may not always be available. In order to avoid cases where young people are 'stuck' in the larger residential establishments, with a mix of residents that may or may not be compatible to their needs, the lobbying must continue for extending the range of specialist individual placements. One obvious forum is the advisory group that supports the Risk Assessment and Management Support Team. This body consists of senior representatives and heads of service from a variety of agencies across the county and is chaired by a senior education psychologist. Initially this group was tasked to oversee the setting up of the team and to ratify policies and procedures. However, increasingly this has become a forum for practice development discussion.

6. A key member of the health of Children in Care training day and co-presenter of the keynote speech was the psychologist with special responsibility for supporting foster carers. She has a 'gate-keeping' function to access support services for carers and as such is often the key person to refer a carer to the Risk Assessment and Management Support Team. We already have a close working relationship with her on a case-by-case basis, but this could be extended to developing a strategic partnership working on wider issues of service development.

7. I would additionally seek to incorporate a fact-finding analysis of resources in other regions of the UK into the discussion document. There are projects in existence that have pioneered treatment foster care: Barnardo's, for example, operates nine projects in England and Wales for children and young people with sexually harmful behaviour, two of which are specialist fostering services. This additional expertise that can be drawn upon will further strengthen and underpin the lobbying and so promote a climate for change.

ACTIVITY **4.6**

- *What are the key areas of legislation related to young people who exhibit sexually harmful behaviour?*

- *How do your professional social work values enhance your capacity to work with young people who exhibit sexually harmful behaviour?*

References

Abbott, D, Morris, J and Ward, L (2001) *The best place to be: Policy, practice and the experiences of residential school placements for disabled children*. York: Joseph Rowntree Foundation/York Publishing.

Aldgate, J, Jones, D, Rose, W and Jeffrey, C (eds) (2006) *The developing world of the child*. London: Jessica Kingsley Publishers.

Aldridge, J and Becker, S (2003) *Children caring for parents with mental illness: Perspectives of young carers, parents and professionals*. Bristol: The Policy Press.

Adoption and Children Act 2002.

Ahmed, M (1995) Enforcement measures winning battle for resources. *Community Care*, 1564, 16–17.

Allen, A (2001) *Making sense of the Children Act*. 3rd edition. Chichester: Wiley.

Andersson, G (2004) Family relations, adjustment and well-being in a longitudinal study of children in care. *Child and Family Social Work*, 10(1): 43–56.

Archer, C (2004) *Next steps in parenting the child who hurts: Tykes and teens*. London: Jessica Kingsley Publishers.

Aries, P (1996) *Centuries of Childhood*. London: Pimlico.

Association of Directors of Social Services (ADSS) (1997) *Children and Families Committee. The foster care market: A national perspective*.

Audit Commission (1996) *Misspent youth: Young people and crime*. London: HMSO.

Audit Commission (1998).

Bambrick, M and Roberts, GE (1991) The sterilization of people with a mental handicap: The view of parents. *Journal of Mental Deficiency Research*, 35(4): 353–63.

Banks, S (2001) *Ethics and values in social work*. 2nd edition. Basingstoke: Palgrave.

Batty, D (2005) Children's services: The issue explained. *Guardian*, 18 May 2005, p7.

Beckett, C and Maynard, A (2005) *Values and ethics in social work*. London: Sage Publications.

Ben-Arieh, A (2000) in Vecchiato, et al. (eds) *Evaluation in child family services*. New York: Aldine de Gruyter.

Ben-Arieh, A (2002) Outcomes of programs versus monitoring well-being: a child-centered perspective, in T Vecchiato, AN Malveccio and C Canali (eds) *Evaluation in child and family services*. New York: Aldine de Gruyter.

Beresford, B (1994) Resources and strategies: How parents cope with the care of a disabled child. *Journal of Child Psychology and Psychiatry*, Vol. 35, pp171–209.

Beresford, B and Lawton, D (1983) *Coping with the care of a severely disabled child*. York: University of York.

Beresford, P, Bowden, J, and Harrison, C (1996) *'What has disability got to do with psychiatric survivors?' Speaking our minds: An anthology of personal experiences of mental distress and its consequences*. Basingstoke: Macmillan.

Beresford, B, Sloper, P, Baldwin, S and Newman, T (1996) *What works in services for families with a disabled child?* Ilford: Barnado's.

Berridge, D (2000) *Placement stability, providing stability and continuity for looked after children is essential for their personal development and achievement*. Luton: University of Luton.

Biehal, N, Clayden, J, Stein, M and Wade, J (1995) Prepared for living? A survey of young people leaving three local authorities. London: National Children's Bureau.

Bierens, H, Hughes, N, Hek, R and Spicer, N (2007) Preventing social exclusion of refugee and asylum-seeking children: Building new networks. *Social Policy and Society*, 6, 219–29. Cambridge: Cambridge University Press.

Blair's speech (2006) *Guardian*, 16 May.

Blaxter, M (1990) *Health and lifestyles*. London: Routledge.

Brassard, J (1982) *The ecology of human development*. Cambridge: Harvard University Press.

Brayne, H and Carr, H (2003) *Law for social workers*. 8th edition. Oxford: Oxford University Press.

Brayne, H and Carr, H (2005) *Law for social workers*. 9th edition. Oxford: Oxford University Press.

Brayne, H and Carr, H (2005) *Law for social workers*. Oxford: Oxford University Press.

Brayne, H and Martin, J (1999) *Law for social workers*. London: Blackstone.

Brechin, A (2000) The challenge of caring relationships, in Brechin, A, Brown, H and Eby, MA (eds) *Critical practice in health and social care*. London: Sage Publications, pp141–61.

Bromfield, C (2000) Why do children misbehave and what can we do about it? Classroom management strategies. Special Educational Needs conference. Bournemouth.

Bronfenbrenner, U (1979) *The ecology of human development*. Cambridge, MA: Harvard University Press.

Cairns, C (2002) *Attachment, trauma and resilience: Therapeutic caring for children*. London: British Associaton for Adoption and Fostering (BAAF).

Calder, MC and Hackett, S (2003) *Assessment in childcare. Using and developing frameworks for practice*. Lyme Regis: Russell House Publishing.

Cameron, A and Lart, R (2003) Factors promoting and obstacles hindering joint working: A systematic review of the research evidence. *Journal of Integrated Care*, 11 (2).

Carroll, M (2001) The spirituality of supervision, in Carroll, M and Tholstrop, M (eds) *Integrated approaches to supervision*. London: Jessica Kingsley Publishers, 76–91.

Cassidy, J (1999) The nature of the child's ties, in J Cassidy and PR Shaver (eds) *Handbook of attachment theory, research and clinical applications.* New York and London: The Guilford Press.

Cemlyn, S (1995) Traveller children and the State: Welfare or neglect? *Child Abuse Review*, 4, 278–90.

Chapel, Dr H-J (1993) *Health and health care needs of travelling families.* Cornwall: Cornwall and Isles of Scilly District and Family Health Services Authorities.

Churcher, M (1996) Challenges in midwifery care: Midwifery care for travellers. *Nursing* 5 (41), 21–32.

Children Act 1989.

Children Act 2004.

Children Act Report 2000.

Chinnery, B (1990) Disabled people get the message: Non-verbal clues to the nature of social work. *Practice*, 4 (1): 49–55.

Cicchetti, D and Rizley, R (1981) Developmental perspectives on the etiology, intergenerational transmission and sequentiae of child maltreatment. *New Directions for Child Development*, 11, 31–5.

Clements, L (2006) The treatment of children under the asylum system – Children first and foremost? *Web Journal of Current Legal Issues* (2006) **http://webjcli.ncl.ac.uk/2006/issue5/clements5.html** (accessed 29 January, 2009).

Clements, P and Spinks, T (2003) *The equal opportunities handbook*. London: Kogan Page.

Coffield, F (2004) *Right brainer or left brainer? Pragmatist or theorist? Research warns against stereotyping people on the basis of their learning styles.* London: Learning and Skills Research Centre.

Collet, J (2004) Immigration is a social work issue, in Hayes, D and Humphries, B (eds) *Social work, immigration and asylum.* London: Jessica Kingsley Publishers.

Common Framework of Assessment 2000.

Community Care (2005). News in Brief. *Community Care*, 9, 14–20 July.

Convention on the Rights of the Child 1991.

Cooper, J (2000) *Law, rights and disability.* London: Jessica Kingsley Publishers.

Corby, B (2000) *Child abuse, towards a knowledge base.* Buckingham: Open University Press.

Cornwall Social Services (2005) Cornwall Social Services Departmental Plan 2005–2006 (draft) *Positive outcomes – practical measures.* Cornwall: Cornwall County Council.

Cotson, D, Friend, J, Hollins, S and James, H (2001) Implementing the framework for the assessment of children in need and their families when the parent has a learning disability, in J Howarth (ed) *The child's world: assessing children in need.* London: Jessica Kingsley Publishers, pp287–301.

Coulshed, V and Orme, J (1998) *Social work practice: An introduction.* 3rd edition. Basingstoke: Palgrave Macmillan.

CPAG (2009) *Children, poverty and disability.* Available at: **http://www.cpag.org.uk/info/Poverty art icle/Poverty109/disability.htm** (accessed 14 April 2009).

CRE – Commission for Racial Equality (2003) *Briefing on gypsies and Irish travellers.* UK Safe Communities Initiative.

Cull, L and Roche, J (2001) *The law and social work.* Buckingham: Open University Press.

Daniel, BM, Wassell, S and Gilligan, R (1999) *Child development for child care services.* London: Jessica Kingsley Publishers.

Daniel, B, Wassell, S and Gillingham, R (2000) *Child development for child care and child protection workers.* London: Jessica Kingsley Publishers Ltd.

Daniel, P and Ivatts, J (1998) *Children and social policy.* Basingstoke: Palgrave.

Davenport, GC (1989) *An introduction to child development.* London: Unwin Hyman Ltd.

Davis, J and Watson, N (2001) Where are the children's experiences?: Analysing social and cultural exclusion in 'special' and 'mainstream' schools. *Disability and Society*, 17(5): 671–88.

Davis, JM and Watson, N (2001) Countering stereotypes of disability: disabled children and resistance, in M Corker and T Shakespeare (eds) *Disability and postmodernity.* London: Continuum.

DCLG – Department of Communities and Local Government (2006) *Planning for gypsy and traveller caravan sites.* London: DCLG circular 01/2006.

Denney, D (1998) *Social policy and social work.* Oxford: Clarendon Press.

Department for Education and Skills (DfES) (2004) *Every child matters: Change for children.* Nottingham: DfES Publications.

Department for Education and Skills (2005) *Common core of skills and knowledge for the children's workforce. Every child matters: change for children.* Nottingham: DfES Publications.

Department for Education and Skills (2005) *Integrated children's system: A statement of business requirements.* Children's Social Services Local Authority Circular: LAC (2005) 3.

Department for Education and Skills (2006) Improving services to meet the needs of minority ethnic children and families. *Every child matters: research and practice briefings 13.* Nottingham: DfES Publications.

Department of Health and Welsh Office (1992) *The Warner Report: Choosing with care.* London: HMSO.

Department of Health and Welsh Office (1997) *The Utting Report – people like us: The report of the review of the safeguards for children living away from home.* London: HMSO.

Department of Health (1995) *Code of practice for employment of residential workers.* London: HMSO.

Department of Health (1995) *Messages from research.* London: HMSO.

Department of Health (1998) *Modernising social services.* London: HMSO.

Department of Health (1998) *Quality protects.* London: HMSO.

Department of Health (1999) *The government's objectives for children's social services.* London: HMSO.

Department of Health (1999) *Working together to safeguard children. A guide to inter-agency working to safeguard and promote the welfare of children.* London: HMSO.

Department of Health (2000) *Framework for the assessment of children and their families.* London: HMSO.

Department of Health (2000) Assessing the needs of children in need and their families: Practice guidance. London: The Stationery Office.

Department of Health (2000) *Children Leaving Care Act: Regulations and guidance*. London: The Stationery Office.

Department of Health, Home Office, Department for Education and Employment (1999) *Working together to safeguard children*. London: The Stationery Office.

Derdeyn, A (1977) Child abuse and neglect: The rights of parents and the needs of their children. *American Journal of Orthopsychiatry* 47, 377–87.

DfES – Department for Educationand Skills (2003) *The Children Act Report: Creating opportunity, releasing potential, achieving excellence*. London: Department for Education and Skills.

DGLG – Derbyshire Gypsy Liaison Group (2004) *A better road: An information booklet for health care and other professionals*. Chesterfield Borough Council: Derbyshire.

Disability Discrimination Act 1995.

Dobson, B and Middleton, S (1999) *Paying to care: The cost of children's disability*. York: York Publishing Services.

DoH (Department of Health) (2000) *Assessing children in need and their families: Practice guidance*. Norwich: The Stationery Office.

DoH (Department of Health) (2000) Framework for the assessment of children in need and their Families. London: The Stationery Office.

DoH (Department of Health) (2001) Children (Leaving Care) Act 2000: Regulations and guidance. London: DoH.

DoH (Department of Health) (2004) *National service framework for children, young people and maternity services: Disabled children and young people and those with complex health needs.* London: The Stationery Office.

DoH (Department of Health) (2004) *The health status of gypsy travellers in England*. University of Sheffield. London: HMSO.

Dominelli, L (1997) *Anti-racist social work: A challenge for white practitioners and educators*. Basingstoke: Macmillan.

Dowling, M and Dolan, L (2001) Families with children with disabilities – Inequalities and the social model. *Disability and Society*, 16(1): 21–35.

Fahlberg, V (1985) *A child's journey through placement*. London: British Association for Adoption and Fostering.

Farmer, E and Pollock, S (1998) *Sexually abused and abusing children in substitute care*. Chichester: Wiley.

Farrington, D (1997) Human development and criminal careers, in Maguire, M and Reiner, R (eds). *The Oxford handbook of criminology*. Oxford: Oxford University Press.

Fawcett, B, Featherstone, B and Goddard, J (2004) *Contemporary child care policy and practice*. Basingstoke: Palgrave Macmillan.

Fawcett, M (1996) Learning through child observation. London: Jessica Kingsley Publishers.

Fekete, L (2005) *Asylum seekers, welfare and the politics of deterrence*. London: Institute of Race Relations.

Fekete, L (2005) The deportation machine: Europe, asylum and human rights. *European Race Bulletin*. London: Institute of Race Relations.

FFT – Friends and Families of Travellers (2007) *Guide to planning*. Available at: **http/www.gypsy-traveller.org. uk**

Foley, P (2001) The development of child health and welfare services in England (1900–1948), in P Foley, J Roche and S Tucker (eds) *Children in society: contemporary theory, policy and practice*. Basingstoke: Palgrave, pp9–17.

Framework of Assessment 2000.

Freeman, MDA (1995) Children's rights in a land of rites, in B Franklin (ed.) *The handbook of children's rights: comparative policy and practice*. London and New York: Routledge.

Freundlich, M (1998) Supply and demand: the forces shaping the future of infant adoption. *Adoption Quarterly*, 2, 13–46.

General Social Care Council (2002) *Codes of practice for social care workers and employers*. London: General Social Care Council.

General Social Care Council (2005) Specialist standards and requirements for post-qualifying social work education and training: Children and young people, their families and carers. London: General Social Care Council.

Gerald, P (1999) *Gypsies, travellers and the health service: An unhealthy community? The evidence piles up*. Basingstoke: Palgrave.

Gerhardt, S (2004) *Why love matters: How affection shapes a baby's brain*. London and New York: Routledge.

Gill, O and Jack, G (2007) The child and family in context: Developing ecological practice in disadvantaged communities. Dorset: Russell House Publishing.

Gould, J (1998) *What is the autistic spectrum?* Available at: **http://www.nas.org.uk/nas/jsp/polo poly.jsp?a=2620&d=364** (accessed 25 February, 2008).

Government Health Action Zone Initiative.

Gray, J (2003) National policy on the assessment of children in need and their families, in H Ward, and W Rose (eds) *Approaches to needs assessment in children's services*. London: Jessica Kingsley Publishers, pp169–73.

Green, J (2003) Concepts of child attachment. Paper given at the Presidents Interdisciplinary Conference, Dartington Hall, 12–14 September, published in the Rt. Hon Lord Justice Thorpe and J Cadbury (eds) (2004) *Hearing the children*. London: Jordans.

Griffiths, E (2002) *Social work practice with disabled children*. Norwich: Social Work Monographs.

Hackett, S (2001) *Facing the future: A guide for parents of young people who have sexually abused*. Lyme Regis: Russell House Publishing.

Hackett, S and Scott, S (2005) *Working together for children and young people with harmful sexual behaviours*. York: Joseph Rowntree Foundation.

Hackett, S, Masson, H and Phillips, S (2003) *Survey of services for children and young people who have sexually abused others – Services in England and Wales*. University of Durham.

Hales, G (1996) *Beyond disability: Towards an enabling society*. London: Sage Publications.

Harrison-White, G (2002) *A briefing paper on traveller issues*. Cornwall: Cornwall Traveller Education Support Service.

Hindle, D (1998) Growing up with a parent who has a chronic mental illness – one child's perspective. *Child and Family Social Work*, 3: 259–66.

HMIP – Her Majesty's Inspectorate of Prisons (2000) Thematic inspection report: Towards race equality. London: The Home Office.

HMSO (2003) *Every child matters*. Norwich: The Stationery Office.

Holland, S, Faulkner, A and Perez-del-Aguila, R (2004) Promoting stability and continuity of care for looked after children: a survey and critical review. *Child and Family Social Work*, 10(1), 29–41.

Home Office, The (1995) Young people and crime. London: HMSO.

Horwath, J (2001) *The child's world: Assessing children in need*. London: Jessica Kingsley Publishers.

Horwath, J (2002) Maintaining a focus on the child? First Impressions of the framework for the assessment of children in need and their families in cases of child neglect. *Child Abuse Review*, 11, 195–213.

Howe, D (2001) in J Horwath (2001) *The child's world: Assessing children in need*. London: Jessica Kingsley Publishers.

Howe, D (2005) *Child abuse and neglect: Attachment, development and intervention*. Basingstoke: Palgrave Macmillan.

Howe, D, Brandon, M, Hinnings, D and Schofield, G (1999) *Attachment theory, child maltreatment and family support: A practice and assessment model*. Basingstoke: Palgrave.

Hudson, B (2000) Inter-agency collaboration – A sceptical view, in A Brechin, JH Brown and MA Eby (eds) *Critical practice in health and social care*. London: Sage, pp253–275.

Hughes, DA (2004) *Building the bonds of attachment: Awakening love in deeply troubled children*. Oxford: Rowman & Littlefields Publishers.

Hughes, N, Hek, R and Spicer, N (2007) Preventing social exclusion of refugee and asylum-seeking children: Building new networks. Social Policy and Society, 6, 219–29. Cambridge: Cambridge University Press.

Human Rights Act 1998.

Humphries, B (2003) *What else counts as evidence-based social work?* Vol. 22. Carfax Publishing. Copyright Taylor & Francis Ltd.

Humphries, B (2004) An unacceptable role for social work: Implementing immigration policy. *British Journal of Social Work*, 34, 93–107.

Jack, G (1997) An ecological approach to social work in families. *Child and Family Social Work*, 2, 109 –20.

Jack, G (2000) Ecological influences on parenting and child development. *British Journal of Social Work*, 30, 703–20.

Jack, G (2001) Ecological perspectives in assessing children and their families, in J Horwath (ed.) *The child's world*. London: Jessica Kingsley Publishers.

Jack, G and Gill, O (2003) *The missing side of the triangle. Assessing the importance of family and environmental factors in the lives of children*. Ilford: Barnardo's.

Jack, G and Jack, D (2000) Ecological social work: The application of a systems model development in context, in P Stepney and D Ford (eds) *Social work models, methods and theories*. Lyme Regis: Russell House Publishing.

Jackson, L (2005) *Region rises to the challenge*. Poole: Bournemouth University. Available at: **http://society.guardian.co.uk/children/story/0,,141502800html** (accessed 26 May, 2006).

Jackson, S and Thompson, N (1999) *On the move again?* Ilford: Barnardo's.

Jenkins, M (2006) *No travellers*. Bristol: Midirs.

Johnson, C and Willers, M (2004) *Gypsy and traveller law*. London: Legal Action Group.

Johnson, S, Cooper, C, Cartwright, S, Donald, I, Taylor, P and Millet, C (2005) The experiences of work-related stress across occupations. *Journal of Managerial Psychology*, 20(2): 177–87.

Jones, C (2001) Voices from the front line: State social workers and New Labour. *The British Journal of Social Work*, 547–62.

Jordan, B (2001) Tough love: Social work, social exclusion and the third way. *British Journal of Social Work* 31, 527–46.

Kelly, G and Gilligan, R (2002) Issues in foster care. Policy, practice and research. London: Jessica Kingsley Publishers.

Kemshall, H (1998) *Risk in probation practice.* Aldershot: Ashgate.

Kemshall, H (2001) *Risk assessment and management of known sexual and dangerous offenders*. London: Home Office Policing and Reducing Crime Unit.

Kiddle, C (1999) *Traveller children: A voice for themselves*. London: Jessica Kingsley Publishers.

Kidner, P (2002) A management perspective, in H Martyn (ed.) *Developing reflective practice, making sense of social work in a world of change.* Bristol: The Policy Press, pp200–11.

Knowles, MS (1990) *The adult learner: A neglected species*. 4th edition. Houston, TX: Gulf.

Kohli, R and Mather, R (2003) Promoting psychosocial well-being in unaccompanied asylum-seeking young people in the United Kingdom. *Child and Family Social Work*, 8(3): 201–12.

Kohli, R and Mitchell, F (eds) (2007) *Working with unaccompanied asylum-seeking children: Issues for policy and practice*. Basingstoke: Palgrave Macmillan.

Korensen, M (1993) Descriptive study of foster and adoptive care services in a Scottish agency. *Community Alternative*, 5 (2): 126–8.

Laming, Lord (2003) The Victoria Climbié inquiry, summary and recommendations.

Laming, Lord (2009) *The protection of children in England: Progress report*. London: The Stationery Office.

Lane, J and Ouseley, H (2006) We've got to start somewhere: What role can early years services and settings play in heping society to be more at ease with itself? *Race Equality Teaching*, Spring.

Liberzon, I (1999) Brain activation in PTSD in response to trauma-related stimuli. *Biological Psychiatry*, 45 (7), 817–26.

Lieberman, AF (2007) *Early adversity and trauma: Derailing healthy growth* (online video lecture). Los Angeles: Baby Futures Summit. Available at: **http://www.lifespanlearn.org/video** (accessed 25 February, 2008).

Liekerman, H and Muter, V (2005) *ADHD (attention deficit hyperactivity disorder)*. Available at http:// www.net doctor.co.uk (accessed 25 February, 2008).

Lishman, J (1998) Personal and professional development, in R Adams, L Dominelli and M Payne (eds) *Social work: themes, issues and critical debates.* Basingstoke: Palgrave, pp89–103.

Lyons, D, Lopez, J, Yang, C and Schatzberg, A (2000a) Stress level cortisol treatment impairs inhibitory control of behaviour in monkeys. *Journal of New Science*, 20 (20).

Macdonald, G (2001) *Effective interventions for child abuse and neglect, An evidence-based approach to planning and evaluating interventions.* Chichester: Wiley.

Main, M (1984–94) Adult attachment scoring and classification system. Unpublished scoring manual. Berkeley: Department of Psychology, University of California.

Marchant, R (1999) *Listening on all channels: Consulting with disabled children*. Brighton: Triangle.

Marchant, R (2001) The assessment of children with complex needs, in J Horwath (ed.) *The child's world.* London: Jessica Kingsley Publishers.

Mark, DR (1996) The use of genograms to identify intergenerational child abuse, unpublished MPhil thesis, University of Exeter.

Maslow, A (1943) A theory of human motivation. *Psychological Review*, 50, 370–8.

Mason, J, Harrison, C and Pavolic, A (1997) *Working with children and lost parents: Putting partnership into practice.* YPS: Joseph Rowntree Foundation.

McClaughlin, C, Florian, L and Rouse, M (2005) Education election briefing. *Community Care*, 1564, 3–12.

McGaw, S and Newman, T (2005) What works for parents with learning disabilities. *Word.* Ilford: Barnardo's.

Meggitt, C and Sunderland, G (2000) *Child development: An illustrated guide (birth to 8 years).* Oxford: Heinemann Educational Publishers.

Middleton, L (1996) *Making a difference: Social work with disabled children*. Birmingham: Venture Press.

Montgomery, A (2004) Asylum seekers as offenders and victims within the criminal justice system, in D Hayes and B Humphries (eds) *Social work, immigration and asylum.* London: Jessica Kingsley Publishers.

Morgan, R and Lindsay, M (2006) *Young people's views on leaving care: What young people in, and formerly in, residential and foster care think about leaving care.* A Children's Rights Director Report. London: Commission for Social Care Inspection. Available at: **http://www.rights4me.org** (accessed 15 February, 2009).

Morris, J (1998) *Still missing: Volumes 1 and 2, disabled children and the Children Act*. Who Cares Trust.

Mussen, PH, Conger, JJ, Kagan, J, and Hurton, AC (1990) *Child development and personality*. 7th edition. New York: Harper Collins.

Mutch, E (2003) *Stress in parenting a disabled child: Social work monographs.* Norwich: University of East Anglia, pp1–34.

National Foster Care Association (1999) *UK national standards for foster care.* Glasgow.

National Foster Care Association (1999) *Report and recommendations of the UK Joint Working Party on Foster Care*. Glasgow.

National Working Group on Child Protection and Disability (2003) *It doesn't happen to disabled children. Child protection and disabled children*. NSPCC: London.

Newman, T (2002) *Promoting resilience: A review of effective strategies for child care services*. Exeter: Centre for Evidence-Based Social Services.

O'Hagan, K (1997) *Competence in social work practice: A practical guide for professionals*. London: Jessica Kingsley Publishers.

Oliver, J (1999) *Understanding disability: From theory to practice*. London: Macmillan.

Oliver, JE (1993) Intergenerational transmission of child abuse. *American Journal of Psychiatry*, 150, 9, 1315–24.

Olson, R and Tyers, H (2004) *Findings, supporting disabled adults as parents*. York: Joseph Rowntree Foundation.

O'Neale, V (2000) *Excellence, not excuses: Inspection of services for ethnic minority children and families*. London: Department of Health Publications.

Ouseley, H and Lane, J (2006) We've got to start somewhere: What role can early years services and settings play in helping society be more at ease with itself? *Race Equality Teaching*, 24(2): 39–43.

Owusu-Bempah, K and Howitt, D (1997) Socio-genealogical connectedness, attachment theory and child care practice. *Child and Family Social Work*, 5, 107–16.

Paquette, D and Ryan, J (2004) Bronfenbrenner's ecological systems theory. Available at: **http://pt3.nl.edu/paquetteryanwebquest.pdf** (accessed 20 January, 2009).

Perry, BD (2006) *Applying principles of neurodevelopment to clinical work with maltreated and traumatised children*. Available at: **http://childtrauma.org** (accessed 20 February, 2008).

Prior, V and Glaser, D (2006) *Understanding attachment and attachment disorders: Theory, evidence and practice*. London: Jessica Kingsley Publishers.

Pugh R (2000) *Rural social work*. Lyme Regis: Russell House Publishing Ltd.

Quine, L and Pahl, J (1995) Examining the causes of stress in families with severely mentally handicapped children. *British Journal of Social Work*, 15, 501–17.

Quittner, AL, Glueckauf, RL and Jackson, DN (1990) Chronic parenting stress: Moderating versus mediating effects of social support. *Journal of Personal Social Psychology*, 50, 1266–78.

Rogers, A (2004) *Teaching adults*. 3rd edition. Maidenhead: Oxford University Press/McGraw-Hill.

Ruch, G (2006) 'Thoughtful' practice: child care social work and the role of case discussion. *Child and Family Social Work, 2007*, 12, 370–9.

Rustin, M (2004) Conceptual analysis of critical moments in Victoria Climbié's life. *Child and Family Social Work*, 10 (1): 11–19.

Rutter, J (2003) *Supporting refugee children in 21st century Britain: A compendium of essential information*. Stoke-on-Trent: Trentham Books.

Rutter, M, Giller, H and Hagell, A (1998) *Anti-social behaviour by young people*. Cambridge: Cambridge University Press.

Ryburn cited in **Denney, D** (1998) *Social policy and social work*. Oxford: Clarendon Press.

Ryder, A (2004) *Decent homes for all*, The Traveller Law Reform coalition. Available at **www.travell erslaw.org.uk** (accessed 10 October 2008).

Sampson, RJ, Audenbush, S and Earls, F (1997) Neighbourhoods and violent crime: A multi-level study of collective efficacy, *Science* 277, p1–7, in G Jack and B Jordan (1999) *Social Capital and Child Welfare Children and Society,* Vol. 13, 242–56.

Schön, DA (1998) *The reflective practitioner: How professionals think in action.* Aldershot: Ashgate.

Shapiro, DL and Levendosky, AA (1999) Adolescent survivors of childhood sexual abuse: The mediating role of attachment style and coping in psychological and interpersonal functioning. *Child-hood Abuse and Neglect,* Vol 23(11): 1175–91.

Siegal, D (2007) Interpersonal neurobiology: The impact of early relationships and experiences on human growth (online video lecture). Los Angeles: Baby Futures Summit. Available at: **http:// www.lifespanlearn.org/video** (accessed 05.06.09).

Shonkoff, JP (ed.) (2000) *From neurons to neighbourhoods: The science of early childhood development.* Washington, DC: National Academies Press. Available at: **http://site.ebrary.com/lib/ bournemouth/Doc**

Simmonds, J (2007) Telling the stories of unaccompanied asylum seeking children, in R Kohli and F Mitchell (eds.) *Working with unaccompanied asylum-seeking children: Issues for policy and practice.* Basingstoke: Palgrave Macmillan.

Sloper, P and Turner, S (1993) Risk and resistance factors in the adaptation of parents of children with severe physical disability. *Journal of Child Psychology and Psychiatry*, Vol. 34, 167–88.

Smith, P, Cowie, H and Blades, M (2003) *Understanding* children's development. 4th edition. Oxford: Blackwell.

Social Services Inspectorate (1998) *Removing barriers for disabled children: Inspection of services to disabled children and their families.* London: HMSO.

South Coast Solutions (2004) *Parent assessment manual software.* High Wycombe: **enquiries @pamsweb.co.uk.**

Stainton Rogers, W (2001) Theories of child development, in P Foley, J Roche and S Tucker *Children in society.* Hampshire: Palgrave, pp202–12.

Steele, M (2003) Attachment theory and research: Recent advances and implications for adoption and foster care. Paper given at the Presidents Interdisciplinary Conference, Dartington Hall, 12–14 September, published in the Rt. Hon Lord Justice Thorpe and J Cadbury (eds) (2004) *Hearing the children.* London: Jordans.

Stein, ID (1974) *Systems theory, science and social work.* New Jersey: Scarecrow Press.

Stein, M and Wade, J (2000) *Helping care-leavers: Problems and strategic responses.* London: DoH.

Steinberg, L (2005) Cognitive and affective development in adolescence. *Trends in Cognitive Sciences*, 9(2): February, 69–74.

Stepney, P and Ford, D (2000) *Social work models, methods and theories: A framework for practice.* Lyme Regis: Russell House Publishing.

Stone, N (1997) Offending, in M Davies (ed.) *The Blackwell companion to social work.* Oxford: Blackwell Publishers.

Thakker, J, Vess, J and Ward, T (2008) Cultural considerations within risk assessments, in M Calder (ed.), *Contemporary risk assessment in safeguarding children.* Lyme Regis: Russell House Publishing.

Thomas, M and Pierson, J (1995) *Collins Educational Dictionary of Social Work*. London: Collins Educational.

Thompson, N (1997) *Anti-discriminatory practice*. 2nd edition. Basingstoke: Macmillan Press.

Thompson, N (2001) *Anti-discriminatory practice*. 3rd edition. Basingstoke: Palgrave.

Thorne, B (1997) Person-Centred Counselling, in M Davies (ed.) *The Blackwell companion to social work*. Oxford: Blackwell Publishers, pp177–84.

Tilley, K (2008) *NSPCC policy summary: Children who are asylum seekers or refugees*. London: NSPCC.

Treseliotis, J (1999) *The organisation and structure of the fostering services in Scotland*. The Scottish Office Central Research Unit.

Trevithick, P (2002) *Social work practice: Assessment*. London: Palgrave, Macmillan.

Utting, D, Bright, J and Henricson, C (1993) *Crime and the family*. London: Family Policies Study Centre.

Ventners, M (1981) Familial coping with chronic and severe childhood illness. *Social Science and Medicine*, 15A, pp289–97.

Ward, L (2005) Child-unfriendly England served notice. *The Guardian*, 2 March 2005, p15.

The West Briton (5 July 2006) *Race relations fears in gypsy site expansion*. Cornwall Publisher, Cornish Guardian Group.

White, R, Carr, P and Lowe, N (2005) *The Children Act in practice*. 3rd edition. London: Butterworths.

Wilier, M (no date) *Human Rights Act 1998 and its impact on travellers*. London. **www.gypsy-traveller.org.uk**

Wilkinson, R (2005) *The impact of inequality: How to make sick societies healthier*. New York: The New Press.

Wilson, A and Beresford, P (2000) Anti-oppressive practice: Emancipation or appropriation? *British Journal of Social Work*, 30, 553–73.

Wintour, P (2006) Blair admits failing most needy children, *The Guardian*, 16 May.

Yule, W (1992) Resilience and vulnerability in child survivors of disasters, in B Tizard and V Varma (eds) *Vulnerability and resilience*. London: Jessica Kingsley Publishers.

Young Women's Christian Association (YWCA) (2006) *A long way to go*. YWCA Briefings. Oxford: YWCA Policy, Research and Campaigns Department.

Index